ENGE BUT WITHOUT BEING OVER THE TOP. EVERYONE WANTS SOMETHING DIFFERENT
NTICS, CHANGING STYLES EVERY WEEK. HE STILL DOES THAT, AND THE HIGH STREET
THE BIBA GRAPHICS WERE MEANT TO REINFORCE THE ~~~~~~~~~~~~~~~~~~ NOT
PRINT THAT GRAPHIC DESIGNERS WORKING FOR FASHI~~~~~~~~~~~~~~~~~~EING
LE. SO, THE PIECE OF ARTWORK THAT IS COMMISSION~~~~~~~~~~~~~~~~ THE
ING TO MEAN ANYTHING. EDITORIAL STYLE IS MOVING~~~~~~~~~ RAPIDLY THAT THE
AS A HOT NEW MEDIUM AT THE BEGINNING OF THE 1990S. IT ECLIPSED MUSIC, AND
IST NOTION, NOT EVERYBODY CAN AFFORD A $500 COAT BUT THEY CAN SCRAPE THE
I THE REAL LOWEST COMMON DENOMINATOR - FINANCIALLY. IN A RECESSION PEOPLE
AZE "GOING UNDER THE NAME HAZE IS ONE OF THE ADVANTAGES AND DIFFERENCES I
D REPUTATION AS A DESIGNER. IN SOME WAYS THE HARDEST PART IS TO FIND YOUR
"I SEE WHAT WE DO AS DESIGN AND THAT CAN BE APPLIED TO ANYTHING. IT CAN BE
PH, WHAT SOMEONE'S WEARING, WHAT THAT'S GOING TO LOOK LIKE AND WHAT IT'S
OF SHIRTS IN THE UK AND A JAPANESE COMPANY BOUGHT THE STOCK AND RIPPED ME
TO START A COMPANY AND USE MY NAME TO PROMOTE IT, SIMON TAYLOR, SO THEY
. IT'S A BIT OF A BAD PUN, SIMON TAYLOR IN JAPANESE MEANS WESTGATE TEMPLE,
COMPLETELY FRACTURED SO NOW YOU CAN HAVE AN UNDERGROUND THING GOING ON
MON TAYLOR, TOMATO, URBAN RE-ACTION "THE THING THAT BOTHERS ME ABOUT THESE
HEIR WORTH. I CAN UNDERSTAND WHY, BECAUSE THERE'S SO MUCH CRAP OUT THERE.
ON A T-SHIRT BECAUSE A LOT OF THE WORK I'VE PUT ON T-SHIRTS HAS ENDED UP IN
AN RE-ACTION "WHAT'S INTERESTING ABOUT T-SHIRTS AND DESIGNS ON CLOTHES IS
D JAPANESE LADY WALKING AROUND IN A T-SHIRT WITH 'BOOGA' ON IT, HER AND IT
THAT ARE BIG AND IMPORTANT AS WELL AS THINGS THAT ARE SMALL. IT'S THE TIME
S VERY QUICK AND FAST. IT ALWAYS HAS BEEN, BUT IN THE UK IT'S PROBABLY QUICKER
O RELATE TO WHATEVER'S HAPPENING TO US, IT CAN ONLY BE LIKE THAT. IF YOU LOOK
HE WORDS HAVE GOT OTHER MEANINGS FOR OTHER PEOPLE AND AS THEY READ WHAT
AUSE I STUDIED PAINTING AT COLLEGE I FELT THEY'D DONE MY HEAD IN COMPLETELY,
OF SITTING AROUND TALKING AND NEVER DOING IT'S A BUNCH OF PAINTERS, SO I LEFT
DIFFERENT TO THE FASHION INDUSTRY. WHEN YOU REALLY MAKE IT AS AN ARTIST YOU
OF IT. BUT NOW I FEEL I COULD TACKLE THE ART BUSINESS. THE PEOPLE SCARE ME A
J AND YOU'D END UP IN TEARS BUT THAT MADE ME REALLY STRONG AND I KNOW HOW
G." ADAM HOWE "FOLLOWING MY UNEXPECTED RE-LOCATION TO JAPAN I NEEDED AN
YS CUSTOMISED OR CREATED GARMENTS, BECAUSE ACTUAL CLOTHES WERE THE LAST
NARRATIVES THAT WERE THE IMMEDIATE PRIORITY. I DECIDED TO PRODUCE GARMENTS
E IN NUMBERS AND SELL THROUGH A COUPLE OF OUTLETS OWNED BY FRIENDS. THIS
OF FANATICS AND WHAT KEEPS MY GARMENTS DESIRABLE IS THE FACT THAT THEY ARE
UCING SUCH LIMITED EDITIONS THAT THEY INEVITABLY SOLD OUT WITHIN DAYS. ALSO,
E!!" BRIAN BADERMAN "I'M A BIT SCEPTICAL AND I LIKE THE FACT THAT THE DIESEL
A STYLE...I STUDIED ENVIRONMENTAL MEDIA AT THE ROYAL COLLEGE OF ART IN
ABLE TRYING TO BE TOO CLEVER ON A GRAPHIC LEVEL." SILVIA GASPARDO MORO "IF
OSE CONCEPT OF FASHION ACTUALLY MELTS WITH GRAPHICS IN TWO AND THREE
EN THE TWO DISCIPLINES HAS ALWAYS BEEN VERY TIGHT." JUDY BLAME "THE WHOLE
DESIGNER, MUSIC, MY OWN LINE, GRAPHICS - THAT'S WHAT KEEPS ME GOING

Wear me: fashion+graphics interaction.
editor and project co-ordinator **Liz Farrelly.** design and art direction **Angus Hyland, Silvia Gaspardo Moro.** design assistant **Deborah West.** photographers **Ferdy Carabott, Andy Hughes** p18-19/64-65/134-135/204-205, **Nico Schwartz** cover/p2. essay by **Maurizio Vetrugno.** translator **Gilda Williams.** copy-editor **Caroline Roux.** published by **Booth-Clibborn Editions 1995.** printed and bound in Hong Kong by **Toppan Printing.** with thanks to Vicky Hayward, Rachel Scott, Katy England, Takeichiro Morinaga, Debbie Granger, Julian Vogel, Tony Blurton and Four IV, Ferdy, Neil, Syd. Sol LeWitt, courtesy of Lisson Gallery, London. Wolfgang Tillmans, courtesy of Daniel Bukhholz, Cologne. Maurizio Vetrugno, courtesy of Galleria SALES Rome. Gavin Turk, courtesy of Jay Jopling, London. the captions and artwork in this book have been supplied by the entrants. while every effort has been made to ensure accuracy, Booth-Clibborn Editions cannot accept responsibility for errors or omissions, under any circumstances. distributed by **Internos Books,** 12 Percy Street, London W1P 9FB, UK. world distribution by **Hearst Books International,** 1350 Avenue of the Americas, New York, NY 10019, USA. US book trade distribution by **Watson-Guptill Publications,** 1515 Broadway New York, NY10036 (908) 343 4511. **ISBN 1873968 558.** copyright 1995 ©introduction Liz Farrelly. copyright 1995 ©brief notes on the universe Maurizio Vetrugno. copyright 1995 ©Booth-Clibborn Editions. **All rights reserved.** no part of this publication may be reproduced, stored in a retrieval system or transmitted in any form or by any means - electronic, mechanical, photocopy, audio or video recording or otherwise - without prior permission of the copyright owners.

Introduction by Liz Farrelly. *Wear me: fashion+graphics interaction* is about the symbiotic relationship between the graphic designer and the fashion designer. The two are inextricably linked, not only in the conventional creative/client partnership, but because each discipline possesses its own unique visual history and vocabulary.

Signs and symbols are the stock in trade of both worlds. Fashion designers and graphic designers are adept at reading, interpreting and appropriating visual codes. That they stray into each other's territory is proof of just how rich these sources of mutual sampling can be.

Wear me aims to draw out the links between these two worlds through designed output, from the fashion-inspired to the graphic-inspired, through the creation of corporate identities (the label) and visual imagery (the fashion shoot). The linkage isn't linear, but a subtle curve that somewhere along the line joins up with itself. This book traces that curving linkage.

Before attempting to link fashion with its graphic language the context around *Wear me* needs explaining. As a fan of fashion and a commentator on graphic design I've been analysing the ephemera which accompanies my purchases for as long as I've been impressed by shiny carrier bags frothing with tissue paper. Based in London I am surrounded by the evidence of sartorial individuality, so that when it came to making a selection of work for this book I aimed to mix up genres, styles and attitudes. From the higher echelons of Bond Street to market stalls in Camden, all levels of the fashion industry are represented. As is made clear in Andy Hughes' photography which graces the chapter openings, they all merge right here on the streets of London, arguably more so than in any other location on this planet.

Material for *Wear me* was sourced by various means; through sending out a call for entries to graphic designers in the UK, Europe and the US; following up leads gleaned through meetings, conversations, and, shopping; and by introducing myself to those members of the fashion community who sounded genuinely intrigued by the project. Along the way I discovered how one of the world's major industries can also lay claim to being a prime outlet for cultural and personal expression.

Even though the majority of work shown here has a connection to London the aim of *Wear me* is not to foreground one city. Globalisation of communication, the media and distribution systems ensure that US labels are consumed in Osaka, clothes designed in Paris are made in Italy and French art directors shoot catalogues for Japanese clients in the London suburbs. Peculiar to the fashion industry is the international exchange of skilled personnel. Photographers, stylists and graphic designers are constantly on the move between clients, magazines, locations and catwalk shows. London is a centre for the creative industries and therefore a great place to sample ideas, so that many clients look no further for services and inspiration. And that *Wear me* was "made in London" has given the selection a particular slant.

The first chapter, Streetlife, concentrates on fashion designers who produce graphics. Having recognised the power of graphics, words or symbols constitute a major element of any garment they produce. Some trained as artists and see designing a collection and producing promotional material as all part of the same process. Others are happy to collaborate with like-minded graphic designers who help them fully realise their ideas. What they all have in common is a respect for the influence of the street and the belief that fashion comes from individuals, not marketing departments. The study of popular culture has proved to them that fashion filters up from the street to the couture houses more efficiently than it filters down, thanks to the energy of youth-oriented media.

Nothing is considered more street than a t-shirt bearing words, whether it's selling beer or whispering anarchy. These Streetlife designers have refined the imagery of the in-your-face attitude of the slogan shirt to the point where other street references – sportswear, graffiti, obvious sexuality – have been incorporated and are now read as fashion. Music-influenced styles from punk to hip hop, babe culture and sports crazes, like skating, surfing, snowboarding, cycling and football chic, all depend on the word for recognition, and all have been appropriated by the avant-garde and mainstream fashion alike. On the most refined level, garments have become symbols of themselves, like two-dimensional pictograms.

Victimisation, chapter two, is full of evidence that it can be fun, even life-enhancing, to be victims, as we all are to a greater or lesser extent, of the power of the label. Fashion victims are easily spotted, but in a consumer society, where freedom of choice is almost a religion, we express preferences over not only what we put on our backs, but also where and how we shop, how we take advice on what to wear and what we wouldn't be seen dead in. But those choices aren't made in a void. We are easily influenced, and it is the job of the graphic designer to package that promise and create label loyalty by means of promotional material.

A fashion designer, or industrial clothing giant, may commission graphics direct or through a PR agent, or employ designers in-house. Scale varies enormously in this industry, but the aim is the same – to produce added value. Packaging may be just that, a box or bag. Although the average punter may never see an invitation to a catwalk show, it could spur a journalist or buyer to filter their approval to a wider audience. Bags, tags, point-of-sale material, product catalogues, postcards, show cards and various freebies are the output of graphic designers working in fashion.

The collaboration gets closer in chapter three, borrowing the title of a Kevin Ayers song, You can take your dream back home. Art direction, whether by a graphic designer or stylist, is crucial for the creation of an image which will sell that dream into our wardrobes. Art directors mediate between the fashion industry and the public by interpreting the raw material (garments) and the philosophy (a fashion designer's vision). The main tool for this interpretation is photography, but the art director will also control exactly how that constructed image will be put to use.

For those graphic designers working independently of any one fashion designer – for a respected magazine, or a younger left-field title – their relationship with the fashion business is mutual dependence. The fashion designers need exposure, the magazines need to fill their pages with seductive or shocking reinterpretations of the meaning of clothes. Magazines can make and break careers, fashion designers can bestow or withhold valuable advertising revenue.

On the other side of the fence are the art directors who act as consultants to particular fashion designers, producing glossy seasonal catalogues. These are reserved for media taste-makers and the most loyal customers, although certain images will be extracted and used in advertising campaigns run in magazines. The stakes in this game are high, necessitating a pledge of extreme loyalty tempered with enough open-mindedness to bring something innovative to the mix, and all on a relentless six-monthly cycle.

What the two strains of art director have in common, and they do stray over the fence, is that it doesn't just end with the image. Creating an interplay between visual and written information reinforces the most subtle of attitudes. And, for the majority of us, the fantasies they help to create for the pages of the monthly style bibles or hallowed catalogues is as close as we'll ever get to the cutting-edge of fashion, and the power it embodies.

As graphic designers get nearer to the source, and begin to understand the control which the fashion industry has over the popular imagination, some decide to grab a part of it. They have become the Talisman makers. Graphic-turned-fashion designers possess the advantages of understanding the power of signs and knowing how to make them. In some instances they work the trick on themselves, employing the language of fashion to enhance their own image, in order to promote themselves to a visually literate peer group within the graphics world and further afield.

This last chapter features work not only by graphic designers, but by others trained as illustrators, fine artists specialising in textiles, and jewellers, all of whom create objects heavily encoded with personal systems of belief. Another sub-section of Talisman makers are those who mediate between the public and various creative industries and sub-cults, be it music, advertising or the club scene, by creating either an oblique language or subverting the common language of logos into sly references. Involuntarily doing a double-take at a t-shirt whose wearer walks past you on the street means that something confusing, private or elitist is happening in a public arena. The work in this chapter differs from the contents of Streetlife in that the message and its impact, not the garment itself, is paramount. The Talisman makers have gone beyond clothing, beyond fashion.

In the contemporary urban environment we are surrounded by logos, statements and graphics, most of which shout an advertising message at us. As the stylist Judy Blame points out, "It's all information", whatever medium we consume it through. Images, words, signs and symbols are, thanks to digital technology, easily appropriated, for whatever purpose and by whoever has the desire and means to do so. This is one way that graphic designers are invaluable to the fashion industry: as disseminators of consciousness-forming images and packagers of mass-produced goods they are a crucial cog in a big business. At the other extreme, as collaborators and subversives working with individual fashion designers or out on their own, they are using one of the most powerful tools of communication, the body, and inscribing their message upon it for all to see. Wear me: fashion+graphics interaction intends to show how the one extreme needs the other; and how, these days, commercialism and opposition cannot be cleanly separated.

How to use this book. Captions on the right-hand page relate to the images on that double-page spread, read left to right. The grey text is either; an extract of "text" from the featured object, a "quote" from an interview, or a "comment" on the project.

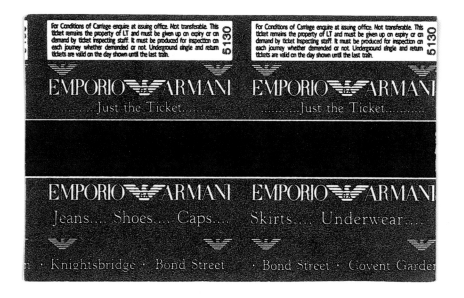

comment "Emporio Armani celebrated the opening of another shop in London by blitzing commuters with their logo on mini-billboards."

There's only one pullover
this photograph
should be used to sell.

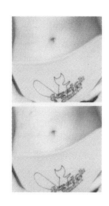

project double-page spread from *Global Vision United Colors of Benetton*. **comment** "the fashion industry is big business. What it needs is a friendly face." **project** pullover press ad and poster. **art director** Andy Dibb. **copy writer** Gary Knight. **photographer** Dave Stewart. **typographer** Kim Le Liboux. **comment** "advertising agency WCRS appropriated a Benetton ad for the AIDS charity, Act-Up London. Media coverage of the outcry against the infamous Benetton campaign ensured that WCRS could drive home their message using an image originally intended to sell knitwear." **project** Moët et Chandon bowler hat. **designer** Judy Blame. **photographer** Marc Lebon. **stylist** Judy Blame. **hair** Daniel at Cuts. **make-up** Paul Star. **comment** "a one-off bowler by designer/stylist Judy Blame was shown in *i-D* no 57 April 1988. In this instance the appropriation wasn't appreciated and Moët sued." **project** identification program for San Francisco Clothing. **designer/photographer/illustrator/typographer** George Tscherny. **design company** George Tscherny Inc. **client** San Francisco Clothing. **year** 1987. **comment** "the graphic language of the street applied to street fashion." **project** Biba logo. **designer** John McConnell. **client** Biba. **year** 1963. **quote** John McConnell "the graphics were meant to reinforce the idea of sumptuousness, not the throw away. It was about Chanel for kids." **comment** "Biba was the first high street fashion retailer to give their customers up-to-the-minute design and a large dose of fantasy to accompany the shopping experience. John McConnell used the language of haute couture to add value to a newly invented marque." **project** Kylie Minogue 1994 catalogue. **designers** Mark Farrow, Rob Petrie, Phil Sims. **design company** Farrow/Dolphin. **client** Deconstruction. **photographers** Ellen Von Unwerth, Katerina Jebb. **comment** "a limited-edition, promotional catalogue for singer Kylie Minogue follows the codes of a fashion catalogue, using a respected fashion photographer and oversized format, turning Kylie into a super model with an array of different looks." **project** Emigre hat t-shirt. **designer** Rudy VanderLans. **design company** Emigre. **year** 1993. **project** press ad. **art director/designer/typographer/stylist** Gerard Saint. **design company** Big-Active Limited. **year** 1995. **photographer** Jocelyn Bain-Hogg. **project** unedible undies included in *phk3* magazine. **designers/illustrators/typographers** Marieke Stolk, Cindy Hoetmer. **design company** PHK-Amsterdam. **year** 1995. **photographer** Marieke Stolk. **comment** "three examples of graphic designers using items of clothing for self-promotion. The Homburg has become Emigre's trademark, bringing an air of tradition to the computer font factory. Big-Active's self-publicity appeared in *Another*, the magazine they design, with the donkey jacket inferring that Big-Active are hard working, down-to-earth designers. The cheap and nasty knickers are designed to shock,just one tactic PHK employ, another is producing a magazine called *period*." **project** photograph. **published in** *i-D* no 107 August 1992. **page nine**

Brief notes about the universe by Maurizio Vetrugno. Fashion is meant to watch and be watched. Over the distance separating these poles of vision one might find the meaning of fashion, that is, its ability to be put into words and stand as the object of discussion. Ancient societies such as the Egyptians witnessed grand eras of catwalks lasting over thirty centuries without any major stylistic variations; it is likely that for them there was little need to analyse the question of fashion.

The invariability of dress codes before they became a matter of law was assured by language itself. It might also be true that all those societies wherein cultural exchange was enacted via a non-alphabetic language were less driven by the need for a meta-language to regulate their course.

For us it is likely that those who decide what to wear one or more times a day, selecting items from a wardrobe, do something quite similar to those who formulate statements picking words out of a dictionary. Apart from our knowledge of it, a dictionary is there physically to be opened by whoever wants to open it, even just to formulate basic statements like "I'm hungry' or "I'm tired", or perhaps to play at the "Exquisite Corpse". Such a dictionary is not, however, for sale at a used book shop.

On the other hand if words had a single meaning and direction – the one ratified by the dictionary – then there probably could be no communication. If clothes are a sign or a set of signs, then one can follow the opposite route and read the signs as a deliberate indication of meaning and behaviour. One can arbitrarily fix the beginning of a prehistory of the signs at hand by referring to the mythological history of Giotto. The story goes that Giotto eliminated all the competition for a major commission when, upon being asked to demonstrate his mastery, he traced a perfect circle freehand with a single stroke. However spurious this might sound, history reminds us that "O" is a circle, the letter "O" and also the number "0".

The Giotto myth reminds us that a sign has multiple primary meanings, and that, arbitrarily fixed, it is also the vehicle for various meanings, the object of other readings and a variety of interpretations.

Before Gutenberg invented his printing press, scribes prided themselves in lingering upon the self-perpetuating aesthetic quality of the page, having it state, without the risk of ambiguity, that the recorded writings of words were not merely the technical, habitual fact of stating words to others. Initial letter illuminations seem to represent the first step toward the evolution of a global communicative aim, emphasising the importance of decoration along the lines of Giotto's circle. That is, if everyone thinks they know something, then the sound of the letters of the alphabet

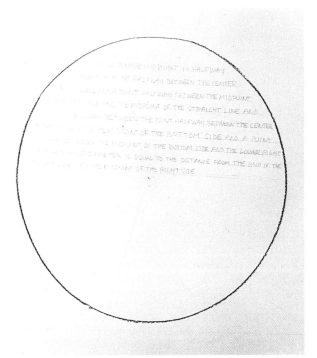

become signifiers/significants, microcosms of visual information, symbols and summaries of giant narrative cycles.

After Gutenberg, individuals such as Giambattista Bodoni hailed a fundamental change. With him we see a path open toward the idea that *what* you say isn't enough; what matters is *how* you say it.

The feeling of Bodoni's publications, his relative indifference to the proof-reading of classic texts, and the way he never worried much about which texts were chosen nor how they were distributed, made him a pure architect of typography – an artist interested in the "hows", the aesthetic side, with an instinct rather than an understanding of the "whats" and the "whys" of the predominant pragmatic or scientific approach.

Laurence Sterne in *The Life and Opinions of Tristam Shandy* created the first modern masterpiece, before the Russian Formalists and the Czech Structuralists. A precursor to Apollinaire and William Burroughs, Sterne amused himself with narrative marks purely in terms of graphics. Here was a text which, from a graphic artist's point of view of Gutenberghian co-ordinates, can bend and wave into rising and falling curves and segments, and in doing so settle for the predictability relentlessly forced upon it by the horizontal, left-to-right arrangement. His narrative summaries are perfect visualisations of the discontinuous nature of the attention paid to facts in the unfolding of events or the impossibility of language to express all of reality through the alphabet.

In the century of light and clarity it became apparent that concepts could be communicated via images in addition to words. In fact, the better we become at manipulating spoken and printed words, the more they prove inadequate for expressing and identifying the multiple perspectives of thought. They are often contemporary and yet at the same time unparalleled, anything but horizontal, not at all foreign to the ghettos of time and space.

The prototypes for the first fashion magazines came about with the spread of courtly frolicking under Louis XIV. With his passion for decoration (he was the real royal decoration freak), the Sun King brought to life paintings which completely changed all styles and dress on a regular basis, depending on his whim and the seasons, lighting the fuse for what we could define as a style, and the virus for the process of planned obsolescence of clothes which is both the beginning and the end for the concept of fashion. Magazines followed this process, consolidating the first nucleus of a system of multiplying images through their reverberation, glorification and even satire, raising the stakes in the social game of emulation which is clearly also a system for control.

By supplying a light and aristocratic yet full-time occupation to the nobility called to court, one multiplied symbolically the image of the king and usurped time and land. Thus, codified spaces were created between areas of controlled freedom and areas of deprivation so that certain materials (ermine) and certain skills (particular embroidery techniques) could no longer be worn by just anyone.

It was the task of court craftsmen to ensure that the desires of abundance and worldly glory could be achieved. Thus, tailors, embroiderers, glovemakers, perfumers and jewellers were gathered together and acquired wealth, power and prestige, laying the basis for jobs effectively tied to the needs of a direct clientele.

The acceleration toward pomp and splendour was embodied in the most extreme and deliberate way in the *Petit Maîtres*, French eighteenth-century libertines, and the Macaronis, their English counterparts. In this case, however, the stakes were different, shifting toward a symbolic level of polemic and a denial of the flow of history. Recently the same fixation on regalia in Vivienne Westwood's work can be read in this sense, as the virulent return to the true origin of the concept of fashion. Before, there had only been costumes; re-reading inverted mythological representations is a constant strategy in her work.

The rhetorical repertoire of names which we have inherited of designers, artists and those arbiters of taste who left an indelible mark on the fashions of their times, coincides historically with the rise of the middle classes, a period when craftsmen with ability to supervise machinery could acquire creative merit. Towards the end of the eighteenth century, around the time of the French Revolution, two separate and emblematic phenomena emerge: Rose Bertin and the *Incroyables*. Bertin was a singular individual whose gaze fell downwards, where no-one had looked before. The Incroyables were a collective whose aim was apparently directed upwards – although actually they looked elsewhere. Their actions crossed paths and created a space which had not previously existed – a no-man's land, the echo box of the demi-monde, the indispensable space to spread fashion, the site of the cycle of death and rebirth.

Up until that final segment of the seventeen hundreds, fashion had been nothing other than the reflection of the king's whims and the court's acquiescent imitation. Rose Bertin (née Marie Jean Laurent) was the first designer whose name has gone down in history. This remarkable fact is due as much to the queen, Marie-Antoinette, who was persuaded by her favourite seamstress to wear clothes which overturned the whole of history by imitating the everyday cottons and wools of ordinary people. But Bertin was exceptional – the only person allowed to enter the gates of Versailles as she pleased without having to show her pass, both literally and symbolically. As Eleanor Lambert has commented,

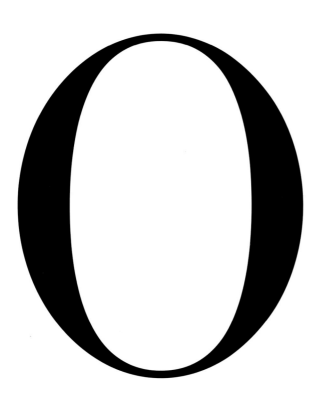

"The queen gave the world popular fashion and the designer's 'name'. The world displayed its gratitude by asking for her head". This is perhaps the first instance in a series to be countlessly repeated – fragments of a discourse. Roman sandals worn by slaves recuperated from the ruins of Pompeii were redesigned by Diana Vreeland; Rei Kawakubo turned Japanese peasant garb into the ultimate in chic on the streets of New York, Paris and London in the early 1980s. The impulse to look elsewhere is part of a cycle which starts in the streets and goes on to influence production which, in turn, influences what is happening in the streets.

Les Incroyables, or Les Merveilleux, were the very first style pirates and certainly the forerunners of a behaviour and attitude for many street stylists to come. They smuggled in signs and poses stolen from the *ancien régime* and then disguised them, exaggerating and often subverting their meaning, secretly succeeding in their aim of revealing the errors and the nonsense which had led to the revolution and the endless spiralling of events of the Reign of Terror. They engraved the buttons of their frock-coats with extremist and irreverent slogans like "Belly free and die", ironically paraphrasing the "Live free or die" of the revolutionaries. Emerging immediately after the execution of Robespierre, their dress and bearing was extraordinarily exaggerated. They walked in tiny, crooked steps and affected lisps. They shaved their necks like those on death row and wrapped huge white scarves, dotted with rust-collared specks or blood-coloured spots to recall those executed, around themselves, half-concealing their chins.

Despite being interpreted as counter-revolutionaries and reactionaries the goal of Les Incroyables wasn't directly political. Their aim was the pursuit of personal amusement and to relish the unease which their presence produced, suggesting that their fight unfolded above all on a symbolic level (although physical conflicts with Jacobeans dressed in carmagnole jackets were for a time an everyday occurrence). Yet in terms of the revolution, they carried out the most poisonous action imaginable: they dissolved the illusion, to reveal the basic unreality of a situation which until then had been accepted, partially explaining why society slid into the terror at all. The revolution had been a dream which turned into the nightmare of the terror. Observing the appearance and disappearance on the scene of the Incroyables helps us delineate one sinuous strand of history.

In simple terms, each time the organisation of a society is about to reach its peak, a sudden style phenomenon arises. There is no warning of its arrival or explanation of its cause. These phenomena seem to spring from nowhere and be directed nowhere, but actually they foreshadow the essential connotations of a society to come. If it's true that Les Incroyables, who, in a period between reigning monarchs gave a sense of what would come in the First

Empire, it was also true for the American Zoot-suiters of the 1940s and the Parisian Zazous during the Vichy government, who prefigured the joyous and carefree attitude of the post-war years. Punks in the late 1970s were precursors of the rise of the free market and the fall of ideologies which followed in the 1980s.

And on to dandies, beaux and bucks in fashion during the endless regency of the Prince of Wales, their elegance lined with cynicism and distance, and the Fashionables, the flamboyants, the *Jeune France*, *abracadabrants*, *gandins*, *lions*, *impossibles*, *cocodés* and *gommeux* of the great romantic period fighting against the bonnets of *coton* and *grisâtres*. Romantics are lined up on one side against the rest of the world, which was rejected as being "bourgeois". On the other side, we find Charles Worth, and we're already propelled into another orbit.

The figure of Worth embodies the true style dictator – the first role model of the fashion system as we understand it today. Worth's primary innovation lay in the creation of clothing which anticipated the new seasons and, above all, in showing it on real live fashion models. This is the first clear indication of the meaning of clothes living primarily through the person wearing them. The amazement and curiosity inspired by his models as they strolled the boulevards of Longchamps contributed to the creation of a new kind of market, aside from giving substance to something that had just been an attitude, which we now know as the demi-monde. Responding to the extreme visibility of his work, the silk-producers of Lyons began weaving fabrics with increasingly interesting surfaces and patterns, and the Empress Eugenia and her ladies were no longer the only ones wearing them. Fashion dolls had been used for centuries to sell fashion. Nearly a hundred years later they remained only as an idiosyncrasy of Madame Vionnet, a genius of Modernist couture who conceived her designs exclusively on miniature mannequins.

Among other things, Worth created the fashion of the padded rear, thus beginning the S-line (Christian Dior in the post-war period made a decisive contribution in nearly completing the rest of the alphabet: the A-line, as well as the Y, I, H, and T lines), but most crucial of all was his thoroughly modern invention of a label, the signature on a dress.

Before it was cause for disease in the 1980s – when those infected became fashion victims – the history of labels had its precursor in the name of Louis Vuitton. The company was the first (under the control of the founder's son George) who, in order to avoid imitation, created a monogrammed *toile* printed with the initials "LV". He was followed by Jean Patou, who chose to put his own monogram on his creations, and then Coco Chanel who used her own initials – the double C. The ever-singular Vionnet left a blank space on her labels after the name to be filled by the print of her own thumb – a bodily stamp which served to authenticate the garment. Thirty years later Yves Klein and Piero Manzoni performed the same act. By expanding the possibilies they ironically authenticated the certainty of being.

In the history of fashion victims it is worth mentioning the Sapeurs who, in an act of self-ironic awareness, chose to wear clothing turned inside out so that the labels of their creators were well in view. On the scene in Paris between 1986 and 1987, their appearance represented the heights this disease could actually reach and they gave rise to the first social antibodies. In this sense Martin Margiela's completely blank label truly represents the bottom line in style: the four visible white stitches on the outside are the abstract representation of the monogram of recognition without the name which can be read inside, which in this case, does not even exist.

The body map - which Belgian designers have recently re-drawn through deconstruction and recycling – had its first re-configuration in a faraway impulse towards the end of the last century, when the severe lines making up the canons of fashion were gradually left behind. The medieval taste in clothing, as it appeared in the paintings of Millais, Rossetti, Holman Hunt and the other members of the English Aesthetic movement at the end of the nineteenth century, predated by some time the fashion for truly aesthetic clothing which encouraged women to assume a more natural manner rather than the wasp waist and prominent bust which the fashions of the times demanded.

Paul Poiret, however, is the man we should credit with having symbolically extended the function of the tea gown, allowing the wearer to loosen the corset or discard it altogether. The tea gown was originally worn for the tea ritual, but was an elaborate garment nonetheless, with long sleeves, a high waist and full back. Replacing all this were Paul Poiret's simple, elegant, flowing clothes which, aside from allowing him to be credited with freeing women from their constrictions, provided a sheet-like bi-dimensionality, an ideal vehicle for the explosion of graphic decoration. A broad range of sources of inspiration were perfect for adaptation: imagery from the Ballets Russes and Klimt, the work of Iribe, Lepape and, above all, Raoul Dufy who designed a great many fabrics for Bianchini-Férier.

Poiret toyed for many years with the basic line created by the corset, but it was Coco (born Gabrielle) Chanel who finally brought about the great de-structuring reform. Of all the technical, stylistic and behavioural innovations which Chanel engendered – the definitive abandonment of the excess of the Belle Époque, the invention of jersey as a fundamental fabric, a feminine wardrobe derived from English menswear – Chanel No. 5 perfume and the introduction of the suntan are the two immaterial offerings which best define her stature. Although it was Poiret who first considered selling perfume as a fashion accessory (his fragrance *Rosina* was named after his second daughter), it was Chanel who gave perfume the guise of aura and allure. Shifting the discourse on the value of aura became all the more evident with the establishment of the tan as an indicator of elegance, energy and health, and opened up myriad discourses for the future. The recent fashion for tattoos and body piercing are just two of the descendants.

Harper's Bazar (which became *Bazaar* in 1913 when Hearst bought it) came into being in 1867. In 1892 Mr Condé Nast's *Vogue* was born. Originally published weekly, and later monthly, these magazines' importance goes well beyond the reconception and updating of feminine illustrated magazines. Through these publications media geniuses such as Alexey Brodovitch arrived on the scene. Brodovitch was *Harper's Bazaar*'s photographer and art director and can be attributed with a large part of its success, against fierce competition from Alexander Lieberman at *Vogue*. Brodovitch left St Petersburg for Paris in 1918. Originally a teacher, in the 1920s he created set designs for Diaghilev's Ballets Russes, as well as textile designs, posters and book and magazine illustrations. He worked in advertising and then moved to the United States, assuming the artistic direction of *Harper's Bazaar* in 1934, eventually becoming one of the great inspirers of style from post-World War II until the present day. He worked with numerous artists and photographers, turning artists into experimental photographers and photographers into the artists behind reproducible and malleable images. His "discoveries" included Man Ray, Robert Doisneau, Irving Penn and Richard Avedon. His many strokes of genius included using the photographs of Moholy Nagy and the optical, graphic tropes of Marcel Duchamp. It is with Brodovitch that Man Ray published his first solarised photographs, a vastly influential technique much in vogue in the 1960s when teams of emulators imposed a mass-stylistic mark on the fashion photography of the day. His influence was immensely broad. Irving Penn, who began as his assistant, once remarked, "all photographers are, whether they know it or not, students of Brodovitch".

The appearance on the fashion scene of the historical avant-garde from the early part of the twentieth century, and once again in the post-war period, gave way to a transformation of specific languages and their multiplication. In terms of energy, one might compare that moment to when, in *The Wizard of Oz*, the film stock changes from black and white to colour. The list of historical avant-gardes and their leading figures belong to a common cultural ground which has been so assimilated as to seem more than obvious, yet nevertheless it continues to be of influence for having prompted the birth of graphics in relation to artistic and creative direction and the dawn of an unprecedented relationship between visual communication and text. Cubism led to the break with all the perpendicular limits of Gutenberg's grid and the one-point perspective of the Renaissance. Surrealism marked the end of the need to communicate a consequential meaning, and introduced the possibility of taking words and discourses apart to rearrange them according to free compositional criteria, in an interaction among various, separate aesthetic languages. Art, fashion, cinema, theatre and poetry co-exist, as do different styles: Picasso with Buñuel and Cocteau; Cocteau with Bérard and Schiaparelli; Man Ray as artist and fashion photographer. Lee Miller photographed reportage from the warfront and images of Chanel learning to sleigh-ride with Cocteau, both for *Vogue*.

Italian and Russian Futurism gave free reign to all onomatopoeias, visual poetry and programmatic manifestos with explosions of form and content which were then freely recomposed: the Futurist reconstruction of the universe by Balla or Depero, who also designed costumes for Diaghilev's "Le Chant du Rossignol"; the hand-painted fabrics of Sonia Delauney; Bragaglia's films with Prampolini's sets. In England the Bloomsbury group of painters, poets and writers creatively redesigned daily life and, as became evident in their painted furniture and household objects, extended their aesthetic vision beyond the printed page and the canvas. Their way of dressing and their life-style was of constant inspiration to the press of the day.

Born in the parallel universe of Duchamp's 1915 star-shaped tonsure, Hugo Ball's wizard's gown of 1920 and outfits made from jelly jars, bird cages, and celluloid by first generation Dadaist Else von Freytag Lohringhoven became legends of freedom only later, as Greil Marcus has noted in *Lipstick Traces*. As gnostic myths of the twentieth century, they were fated never to be acclaimed, or to die out. Where Irene Castle's boyish haircut of 1915 established *the* haircut to have in the twentieth century, Gertrude Stein's sandals and tunic made from rough brown cotton created no immediate feedback. However, these acts had increasing effect, becoming issues of interest well beyond the tight circle which made up their natural public.

In the history of haute couture we can trace the proof of a basic duality or we can at least attempt a dualistic reading of the impulses which, in striving for newness and perfection as aesthetic categories worthwhile in and of themselves, have brought – at least in intent – the creators of fashion to see their creations as statements in relation to an absolute. The line of Modernism in couture, which sees the outfit as an ideal synthesis wherein the classic distinction between design and styling is almost nil, has as its forerunner the primordial androgyny represented by the work of both Mariano Fortuny and Paul Poiret. Their research led to non-structured clothes that reached dizzying heights of decoration – opposites which represent the two constants in this history, not merely opposed but joined together. This is not the case, however, in the obsessions of Vionnet, Chanel and Alix (later known as

Madame Grès).

If Fortuny introduced and re-interpreted the majority of forms, from ethnic outfits to garments made from exotic and extravagant silks, Vionnet's research – like Grès' some time later – reveals a puritan soul, more semiotically than economically. The same spirit behind the birth of design makes it by nature the enemy of fashion and reveals one of the obvious contradictions that feeds the course and recourse of the changing fashion system. Chanel's vocation from the very start was to be minimalist, agreeing with the rationalist credo that "less is more". Increasingly Chanel embodied the figure of the rebel, dictator and reactionary. Vionnet invented and perfected an intricate system of bias cuts and diagonal stitching, and many of her dresses closed up the back or were pulled on over the head with no fastenings. In 1910, while designing for Maison Doucet she introduced her revolutionary one-layer dress, presenting it on barefoot models. It is the very same image which still adorns the bonnet of a Rolls Royce today. From the moment she came on the scene, her work had a particular aesthetic overtone that was later brought to its natural conclusion by Balenciaga during the post-war period, and exhibited the same sense of Modernism as the design of Mies Van Der Rohe and Le Corbusier.

The streamlined, simple elegance of Vionnet, Chanel and Grès was not part of Elsa Schiaparelli's panorama of imagery. Her taste for extremes, shock value and constant invention set her on the other side. Her idea of elegance was a combination of irony and arrogance known as "hard chic". Notable innovations included shocking pink, a colour invented with Christian Bérard to launch her perfume of the same name; the glass dress made of crepe, silk and fibreglass; and the use of the zipper for hyper-fashionable clothes, conspicuously positioned rather than concealed. She worked with Dalì to make hats of all kinds – shaped like an upside-down shoe, an animal's face, an ice-cream cone, or a lamb chop; and with Cocteau to create *trompe l'oeil* embroidery, poetry and calligraphy on capes, and profiles which define the cut of suits. Bérard designed many of his most original prints and colour combinations exclusively for Schiaparelli, while André Perugia, who designed fish-shaped shoes for her, took his inspiration from Picasso and Jean Schlumberger. His graphic surrealism produced pockets with lips, giant lobsters printed on evening dresses, and all sorts of buttons, and precious and costume jewellery. The noted French textiles company of Calcombet produced a fabric for Schiap, as she was known, with a newsprint design, from which she created blouses and scarves. The appearance of words as a found object bearing the effect of reality was first introduced into art by the Cubists. Marcel Duchamp, in his film *Anaemic Cinema*, added an alienating, ironic effect. Now the two had found their way into fashion. Later newsprint was used by Fornasetti, and was destined to expand into many variations and applications.

In the area of high fashion, Yves Saint Laurent slavishly borrowed Schiaparelli's cape in the 1960s with Cocteau's sun and poetry picked out in sequins, but the Situationists had picked up that particular Ariadne's thread ten years earlier and wrote messages on their clothes with more of a tattoo flavour than one of decoration. Lettriste writings later inspired the heyday of message-shirts and badges from the 1960s to the punk explosion of text when Malcolm McLaren and Vivienne Westwood designed punk outfits that perfectly represented the idea of the society of the spectacle described by the Situationists. In the same way the ecological, biting texts on Katharine Hamnett's and Franco Moschino's t-shirts can easily be read as the positive mirror-image of the same phenomenon.

Following the trail blazed by the great structurers of fashion – starting in the 1930s and continuing until the crucial year of 1968 when the final farewell was bid to the atelier – came another personality, Cristobal Balenciaga. In terms of a rhetorical repertoire we can plainly see how Balenciaga's work is what comes immediately to mind when abstractly thinking of high fashion in general. His mad obsession with work, his preference for studying line at the expense of colour (collections were in sober tones, although he was later recognised as an accomplished colourist) and the ascetic and isolated life he led during the thirty years of his dominance, fully warrant that he be part of that ideal genealogy which stems from the aforementioned puritan soul.

Thus the explosive, full-flared line and the so-called alphabet line in Christian Dior's new look in the post-war period to the end of the 1950s, and the introduction of thin, pirouetting-pony models in a world grown accustomed to statuesque models, are but a few of the examples by which one can interpret Dior as belonging to some other universe.

From Jean Patou in Europe in the 1920s and later Claire McCardell in the United States in the 1940s, one can trace the influence of sportswear outside its specific context. Patou's inspiration contributed to the new dimension in clothing for the modern woman, who was active and wanted to look active. He designed clothing for tennis champion Lenglen, who loved to wear his clothes both on and off the court. Similarly Claire McCardell not only followed a minimalist line, and was largely responsible for the success of the waistless, monastic bias-cut look, but also contributed considerably to establishing sportswear as a permanent source of inspiration in the fashion collections of later generations of designers both in Europe and the United States. The sportswear influence reached its peak in the early 1980s, when the body became the new object of attention and led to some interesting interaction: fashion designers made certain sportswear brands trendy, gleaning them from the street and forcing designers of sportswear and related products to consider the fashion content in addition to the clothing's functional qualities.

The end of the 1950s saw the end of traditional haute couture as café society was transformed into the jet-set (although it took at least ten years to settle the bill fully). Then, the beginning of the 1960s saw first the pop explosion, which led to the assertion of street style and related social behaviour happening outside of those cultural groups which had originally produced them. The influence of art was felt in fashion and on the street.

Yves Saint Laurent's mingling of fashion with modern art, like the aforementioned Cocteau cape, the Matisse cut-outs and the famous Mondrian dress from 1965, was not spawned by the bi-dimensional thinking of the drawing table. If these represent the constant ideal of Paul Poiret's discourse, they also show up its limits, the very same effect which became all the more apparent in Lucio Fontana's slashes once they were printed and flattened on Mila Schön's 1967 tunic. This is quite different from the translation of Futurism and the Modernist lessons of the Bauhaus offered by André Courrèges and Paco Rabanne. With them, designs borrowed from Fortunato Depero and Oskar Schlemmer came to life, finally gaining access to the third dimension and bodily movement. But the clothes were far from natural. They took artificiality and obviousness to extremes, particularly in the case of Rabanne who "built" – quite literally – clothes which weighed up to sixteen kilos. Singer Françoise Hardy, an icon of talent throughout the 1960s, wore them in performance but had to be moved on stage with the help of assistants. On the other side of the ocean, Rudi Gernreicht brought the circle to a close by perfecting the invention of the total look, so total as to be embodied fully only by a single model: Peggy Moffitt.

André Courrèges, who began as Balenciaga's assistant, competed with London designer Mary Quant to make the mini-skirt fashionable. The new length set the tone for years to come and, with the frequent appearance of a bull's-eye on the dress front, made the mid-riff the true focal point of the body during the 1960s, as if the energy released during that decade had its origins directly in the belly-button. Courrèges' doll-like clothing was fashioned in synthetic materials, and went well beyond the era of the Lear jet and directly into outer space. "Space Age" remains one of his most famous collections, fated to be reproduced and imitated ad nauseam in every film and television programme bearing any reference to the future. Paco Rabanne, in turn, with the conscientiousness of a craftsman, used any material whatsoever (metal, plastic, feathers), freed from all immediate fashion connotations, to produce an exact parallel to the post-informal research in art at the time. A similar contribution to the Modernist cause was made by Germana Marucelli with her Aluminium collection in 1968, and particularly the Egg Shell dress, a product of her collaboration with Getulio Alviani.

Behavioural influences were seen in Betsey Johnson's silver shell-suit with skeleton print and the minimal influence in Diana Dew's clothes with flashing electric lights. The influence of Bridget Riley and her wavy repeated lines was seen in Federico Forquet; Marc Bohan for Dior and Mary Quant created clothing with optical patterns that suggested movement even on still bodies. Optics were among the influences destined to be cyclically repeated, although never for more than a season at a time. Graphics in any case exploded in all directions, succeeding in its intent to push Pop Art into the world all around it, and thereby creating an odd short-circuit, with Pop returning right back to where its origins were.

In some ways these experiments were on the same continuum as the puritan spirit behind much of the formal research of Vionnet/Chanel/Grès, but with a shift in meaning. Two linked phenomena made the difference. First, the massive rise of prêt-à-porter had forced a global reconsideration of the conception, production and distribution of a product; and second, the rise of the boutique (Granny Takes a Trip, Mr Freedom and Biba in London and Paraphernalia in New York, are but a few examples) as autonomous organisms of taste destined to anticipate or reflect the moods of the street. These manufacturing and retailing innovations echoed the divisions of taste among the growing urban tribes.

Throughout the 1970s, with few exceptions, the effect of individual fashion designers was outweighed by the globalisation of rock stars, who as stylists, had greater resonance. This model was fully exploited during the 1980s with the explosion onto the market of image-makers. At the same time public awareness, of why and how the sophisticated imagery produced in the name of advertising is actually made, has grown and grown.

The symbolic figures *par excellence* during the 1970s and 1980s , with their pure, daring spirit, were Malcolm McLaren and Vivienne Westwood – extraordinary examples of anti-designers fated to act as role-models despite their own intentions. In the various incarnations of their shop, they sold nostalgic items to teddy boys (Let It Rock, 1972); black leather jackets to bikers (Too Fast to Live Too Young to Die, 1973); and sado-masochistic paraphernalia for fetishists and angry youths (Sex, 1974). But they found their definitive momentum as they piloted the punk explosion in the umpteenth transformation of their shop into Seditionaries in 1976. With the emergence of punk, the energy and the audience was for once far more extreme both visually and conceptually than the performers on the scene. Westwood and McLaren always enacted a policy of inverted mythological representation even after they separated. We can find obvious examples in their "Nostalgia of

Mud" collection, and in the parallel launch of the square dance which referred obliquely to "The Rape of the Sabine Women". Later the dance craze of Vogue-ing, with its origins in the darkened recesses of the slums of Harlem in dance halls concealed from the eyes of the world, presented a parody of the fashion magazine; the body was pushed to its limit in positions on a par with voodoo dance rituals. When McLaren referred to the House of Saint Laurent and the dance with one's own shadow in his own Vogue-ing inspired song, he seemed to evoke the night of Saint Lorenzo on 10 August – when dancing with one's own shadow beckons the spirits of the earth – rather than YSL.

STREETLIFE. CATWALK DIFFUSION STREET FASHION. REVELLING IN THE POWER OF COMMUNICATION. GRAPHIC DEVICES AND SIGNS FROM THE URBAN LANDSCAPE

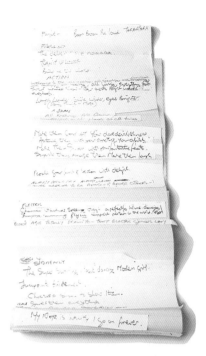

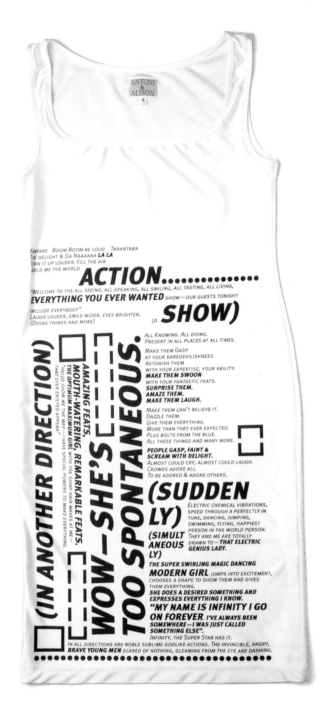

read from left to right. project screen for printing. title be happy collection. designers Antoni Burakowski, Alison Roberts. design company Antoni & Alison. year 1987. project photograph of studio. title modernist/visionary collection. client Antoni & Alison. year 1994. photographer Paul Neale. project cut up writing. title action collection. designers Antoni Burakowski, Alison Roberts. design company Antoni & Alison. year 1995. project the show dress. title action collection. designers Antoni Burakowski, Alison Roberts. design company Antoni & Alison. year 1995. typographers Graphic Thought Facility. quote Antoni "we knew we wanted to work together and we knew when we did the be happy collection for a French fashion prediction company and it was so hated, it caused such a reaction, we thought, this reaction is so interesting. But it was perfect for England, a year later, the whole summer of love thing happened. Basically, we write the collection, from the beginning instead of drawing anything we write it. It was such a brilliant way of describing things. It became more interesting than a pair of trousers or a print you could think of, actually that part of it became the most interesting thing for us. So it was purely about thinking thoughts, wonderful things that would come into your head." quote Alison "the action collection is supposed to literally spur you into action so you really don't have any regrets, and no one knows how long we've got. You kind of think that if there's a pattern in anyone's situation, it's a human nature thing, just maybe if we could spur one person on to do what they've always wanted to do that would be brilliant, but we won't hear about it. I know it's only a dress or a t-shirt, but potentially, because of the communication value, maybe that would happen." page twenty one

IF IT IS THEN. I WANT TO BE HAPPY. I HOPE THAT I HAVE TO. / OH MY GOD. IT'S HAPPENING. GET READY. IT'S HAPPENING THINGS ARE CHANGING. O.K. THEN. BEGIN TO GO. NO. YES, START. GO. / The door is open > Nobody tells you you have to you just know you want to > step inside > you see a ray of light > ultra light > a straight directional light line beaming into the distance > follow that light > suddenly you realize / Oh my God > you are there > it's new > it feels like delicate virtues giving super feelings > your heart becomes pure > it beats honest truths > you have ultra faith > everyone is there to lead the way here on earth in the modern world. Scared of getting there? Enjoy going through it.

fabric samples. **title modernist/visionary collection. designers Antoni Burakowski, Alison Roberts. design company Antoni & Alison. year 1994. typographers Graphic Thought Facility.** project journey to a place called there packaging back card. **title there collection. designers Antoni Burakowski, Alison Roberts. design company Antoni & Alison. year 1994. typographers Graphic Thought Facility.** project vacuum-packed t-shirt. **title action collection. designers Antoni Burakowski, Alison Roberts. design company Antoni & Alison. year 1995. typographers GTF.** project vacuum-packed t-shirt. **title action collection, part of range I find plain exciting. designers Antoni Burakowski, Alison Roberts. design company Antoni & Alison. year 1995. typographers Graphic Thought Facility. quote Antoni** "you do have parts of the collection that go on and on and on, but we put them into the garment, they get them all for free, we turn them into labels that get stitched inside, its all extra things but it's important for us that it's there. No buyer would actually buy it because it's too mad or funny or too going on a bit, and they don't want that, they want, dedadedadeda, and it's like OK, but you have to have this, it's a secret thing. It's placed in with the packaging so when you open it you have this thing and if you want to read it great, if you don't throw it away, fine, it's OK you've made you're decision. We found vacuum packing and that was really brilliant for us. You're thinking about a lot of different things, the aesthetics of it obviously in that you're actually able to see the whole thing, the words. People are buying the words. In Japan it's gone a bit further, people buy them not to even open them, to keep, we feel very happy about that." **page twenty three**

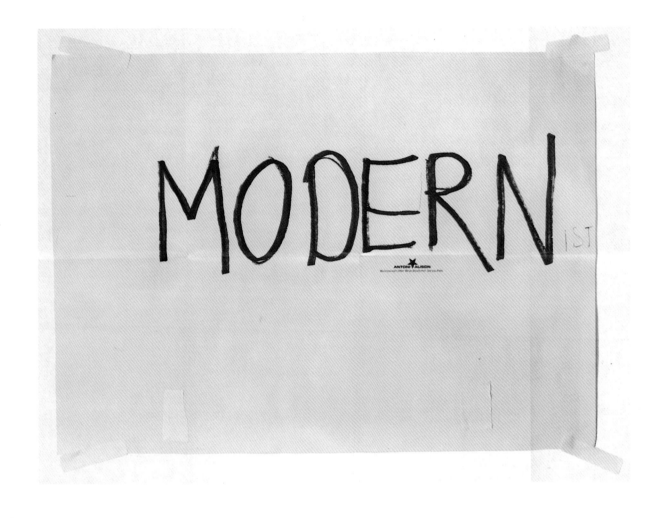

project promotional poster/mail order catalogue. **title action collection. designers/typographers Paul Neale, Andrew Stevens, Antoni & Alison. design company Graphic Thought Facility. client Antoni & Alison. year 1995. photographer Andrew Penketh.** project poster/mail order catalogue. **title modernist collection. designers Graphic Thought Facility, Antoni & Alison. design company Graphic Thought Facility. client Antoni & Alison. year 1994. photographer Andrew Penketh. typographers Antoni Burakowski, Alison Roberts. hair Kerry Warn. make-up Carol Brown. quote Antoni** "a big criteria of our work is this idea that it's modern, not modern in that it's got to be ahead of it's time, but in the fact that, especially the packaging, it's a reference to that time when people were looking forward." **page twenty five**

BRITISH INDUSTRIAL GIANT

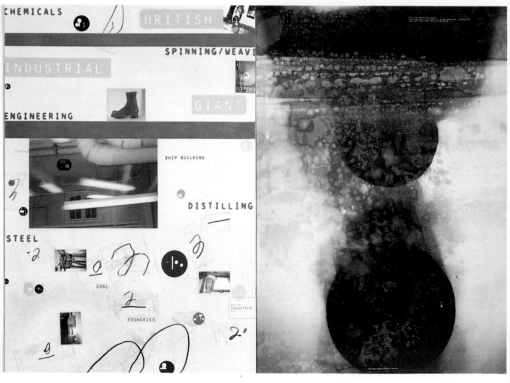

project catalogue. **title British Industrial Giant. designers Dirk Van Dooren, Jonathan Cooke. design company Tomato. client British Industrial Giant. year 1994. illustrator/typographer Dirk Van Dooren. comment** "heavy-duty workwear boots are represented amid relics of industrial decay depicted in a variety of graphic/photographic techniques." **page twenty seven**

beauty:beast

project press photo. **title bent poetry for liquid evenings.** designer Adam Howe. design company Adamuchi. year 1994. photographer/stylist Adam Howe. hair/make-up Hina Dohi. model You Fujimoto. text Adam Howe. "the cruel side to my sense of humour resulted in the collection I called 'bent poetry for liquid evenings'. A couple of fashion students came into my studio to buy some of my old samples, they wanted me to autograph a shirt and I found the idea so ridiculous that I signed it 'Sycophant!'. Of course they didn't know what it meant, but were delighted none the less. So, I produced a range of shirts and t-shirts with printed, stamped text, that began with 'Osaka Heroes' from Mickey Mouse to Sid Vicious, exploring the phenomenon of heroes and fanatics. I included text from Joseph Campbell's 'Hero with a thousand faces', to babbling rubbish which was basically insulting the very people who were buying the product, with lines like, 'Exploit the flock mentality of impulsive youth!' and 'Victim Nationale'.

The second collection was called 'Adamuchi-Gumi', a dig at situations in Japan that were basically nationalistic and xenophobic. I was still seeing if it was possible to shock Japanese teenagers. So, the Adamuchi logo became Adamuchi-Gumi a reference to the power of the Japanese Mafia, Yakuza, the largest group being the Yamaguchi-Gumi. It had the desired effect of being risqué to wear, although in reality the chances of these kids coming into contact with hard-core gangsters was fairly slim. For the rest of this collection I continued to play with typography and slogans, but utilising the Japanese Kanji alphabet. The first design was 'Gaijin no baka ya ro' which literally means 'Fuck off western foreigners', again a dig at Japanese xenophobia.

This somewhat backfired because a lot of Japanese kids wanted them, but the shirt was only amusing if a western foreigner wore it, just as the 'Nigger' shirt, popular in New York, was only ironic if a black person wore it. My solution to this problem was to print on the price tag 'Strictly for sale to Gaijin (westerners) only!' As the response to shirts with Kanji lettering was so good I then produced the tamer flame t-shirt which boldly claimed 'Kyonu dai yon' which is thick Osaka dialect for 'Big tits innit!'." **project collection.** designer Takao Yamashita. design company beauty:beast. **project logo.** **title beauty:beast.** designer/typographer Simon Taylor. design company Tomato. client beauty:beast. year 1994. page twenty nine

project Hysteric Glamour

fashion story. **title** *A Be Sea* **a visual paper, issue f. year 1995. photographer** James Lebon. **publisher/editor** Sebastian Boyle. **project** promotional stickers. **client Hysteric Glamour. agents** Gimme 5 Limited. **year 1995. comment** "Japan-based Hysteric Glamour specialise in producing t-shirts and sportswear emblazoned with irreverently recycled graphic devices, most notably the Playboy logo." **page thirty one**

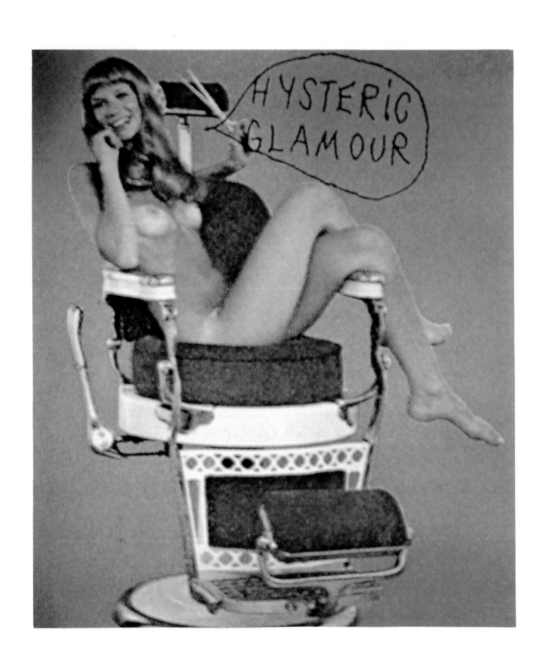

In a collection which shares aesthetic values with the high opulence of the 'Mirage' and 'Flamingo Hilton', country rock glitz is merged with the air-con-cool of V8 Coupe de Villes shimmering under the neon Nevada night as they cruise THE STRIP.
With the attitude of the dealers, the takers and the cowboy angels, cocktails of the finest buck skin and sheer leathers are intricately trashed with rhine stones and glittering tattoo transfers, each piece enticing with the sensual decadence of L.A. rock glamour.
FLAUNT everything and more with the easy Hyper-cool style arrogance of a Winner in SIN CITY...........

Information through MODUS PUBLICITY 071-938 3888

project postcard. client Hysteric Glamour. year 1994. agents Gimme 5 Limited. project catalogue. title the gilded palace of sin. designers/typographers Jane Shepherd, Ian Hebditch. design company Jane Shepherd. year 1994. photographers Ian Hebditch, Peter Hill. stylist Ian Hebditch. model Jane Shepherd. page thirty three

designers Lee Farmer, Daniel Poole. client Daniel Poole. year 1993. photographer Julian Hawkins. illustrator Dennis Dykes. project jacket with bar code. **designer/client Daniel Poole. year 1991. comment** "graphic designer Mervyn Rands works closely with clothing designer Lee Farmer to create a series of graphic icons, commenting on major themes – ecology, tribalism, gheottisation – for each collection. These icons are re-combined into large painted illustrations, by Dennis Dykes, which are then used for advertising and promotional purposes." **page thirty five**

project press photo. designers Lee Farmer, Mervyn Rands. design company Penrose Design Limited. client Daniel Poole. year 1993. photographer Joep Kroes. illustrator Mervyn Rands. project icons on blue linen. designers Lee Farmer, Mervyn Rands. design company Penrose Design Limited. client Daniel Poole. year 1993. illustrator/typographer Mervyn Rands. project packing tape. title world safety systems. designer/design company Daniel Poole. project reflective logos. client Daniel Poole. page thirty seven

project reflective t-shirt. title ghetto culture. designer Lee Farmer. design company/client Daniel Poole. year 1993. project double-page trade ad. title *Sportswear International* european edition fall/winter 93/94. designers Lee Farmer, Mervyn Rands. design company Penrose Design Limited. client Daniel Poole. photographer Sandro Sodano. typographer Mervyn Rands. project retail advertising campaign. title *The Face*, *i-D* ads. designers Lee Farmer, Mervyn Rands. design company Penrose Design Limited. client Daniel Poole Retail Limited. year 1994. photographer Julian Hawkins. illustrator Dennis Dykes. typographer Mervyn Rands. project skateboard. title molecular skate. designers Simon Gunning, Mervyn Rands. design company Penrose Design Limited. client Daniel Poole. year 1994. illustrator Dennis Dykes. typographer Mervyn Rands. page thirty nine

project cover, double-page spread from press book showing spread from *i-D* June 1986. **title Nemeth. designer Christopher Nemeth. photographer Marc Lebon. stylist Fred Poodle at Home. hair/make-up Yvonne Gold. model Sarah Wingate, Z Agency. helping hands Eddie Monsoon.** project jacket. **title hero jacket. stylists Judy Blame, Christopher Nemeth. photographer Marc Lebon. from the collection of Marc Lebon. quote Judy Blame.** "we met because Marc Lebon saw Christopher Nemeth on the street one day and just jumped out of his cab, and went, 'where the bloody hell did you get those clothes from' and Chris went, 'I made them', and Chris was so poor at the time, so Marc went 'can you came round to my studio tomorrow with everything that you've made?'

It was the end of 1984, and he came round with two bin liners full of clothes and I just happened to be there because I'd just met Marc and we were trying to get a good photography/styling thing together. He said, 'you've got to see these clothes'. Chris tipped the bin liners out and all these brilliant clothes fell out and Marc bought all of them immediately, like everything. Chris had left Camberwell School of Art, he was a painter, and the reason he started making clothes was because he was a fine artist and it's so hard to get into fine art circles in London, and he had no way of making money so he started making clothes out of post sacks and his paintings, found things, whatever, and I was making a lot of jewellery at the time out of recycling found objects.

So the minute I saw the clothes, and Marc bought the lot, we started PR-ing Chris and using the clothes in pictures. We started wearing them out and getting people to come and see them, it just took off and because they were so brilliant people reacted. When we first started we literally had to make everything ourselves. It was always Chris' ambition to make the clothes really properly. But he never had the facility of a factory that understood his patterns, and his fabric and his concept, but in Japan he found it. The factories out there are amazing, so the last collection we did in December 1994, it took me and Chris six weeks to put a whole collection together, of 59 full outfits, 380 garments.

We're so well suited, we're kind of like the Laurel and Hardy of fashion, Chris is good at certain things and then I am at others. It's like I said I can't cut a pattern and Chris can. It's not that I'm changing his vision, just expanding it with my knowledge of the fashion business. Chris has been so isolated in Japan but he's built up a big stronghold of kids that buy the stuff. I couldn't believe it how many young kids think Nemeth is god out there, and he's got a really hands on approach about it, it's not elitist. Nemeth might be in the store saying, 'oh no not that shirt this one might be better for you', he's very practical, I'm a bit more kind of aloof." **page forty one**

projects machine-

embroidered denim jeans, painted velvet waistcoat. title spring/summer 1995. designer Christopher Nemeth. stockist Browns. page forty three

project mesh t-shirt with knitted collar. **title spring/summer 1995. design company Jean Paul Gaultier. stockist Browns.** project enamelled logo on fitted jean jacket. **design company Junior Gaultier. private collection London. comment** "the ubiquitous enamel badge applied the form of automotive insignia to clothing." **page forty seven**

project embroidered logo. title John Richmond Mainline. designer David Richmond. design company David Richmond Associates. client John Richmond. year 1993. typographers David Richmond, John Richmond. project printed logo. title Destroy '95. designers David Richmond, David Gray. design company David Richmond Associates. client John Richmond, Destroy. comment "the team of two brothers, fashion designer John and graphic designer David, collaborate on both packaging and garments." page forty nine

Photography Marcus Tomlinson. Car Capri Club International. Another Dave Richmond

project logos/labels. **title Destroy '93. designer David Richmond. design company David Richmond Associates. client John Richmond, Destroy.** project label. **title Richmond Denim. designers David Richmond, David Gray. design company David Richmond Associates. client Richmond Denim.** project press ad/poster. **title Destroy '94. designer David Richmond. design company David Richmond Associates. client John Richmond, Destroy. photographer Marcus Thomlinson. typographers David Richmond, David Hitner, David Gray. page fifty one**

project t-shirt prints. title Destroy
'95. designers David Richmond, David Gray. design company David Richmond Associates. client John Richmond, Destroy. page fifty three

xprstle

The show was held in 1638 in Marince St Germain in a marquee. The dancers had an introduction of their theme published in a newspaper prior to the show."

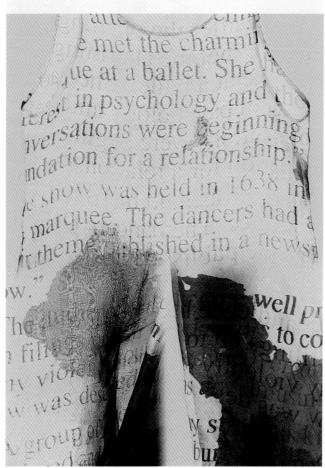

press/publicity photos. title Hussein Chalayan autumn/winter 1994. designer/photographer/typographer Sandro Sodano. design company Aboud Sodano. client Hussein Chalayan. quote Hussein Chalayan. "I wrote a fictional story which related to the collection and printed it on a dress, the clothes symbolise the story. Parts of the story are sewn into garments, it involved you with how the garment evolved, the garment had a history, as labels, facings, back, pockets. Some of the words are hidden in the garment and only the wearer will see them. The garments are also objects that could be put on the wall, that you could look at and read inside, pull things out. The balloon dress was about people who feel they'd be saved in a given situation, like people who jump off buildings and think they'll be saved by an exterior force, jumping off with the balloons, but falling straight down. It's ridiculing that belief, but there is also this feeling of heavenly expectations and weightlessness with the balloon dress." **quote Caroline Roux _Blueprint_ November 1994** "the paper suit creates a visual joke around the traditional nature of the garment type, the avant-garde and (apparently) ephemeral nature of the fabric. The paper itself is actually a non-tearable polyethylene, tradename Tyvek, that's generally used to make envelopes....(Hussein Chalayan) 'It's meant to suggest packaging...I was talking about the horrors of war, and the lack of respect for the individual; how people are just packaged off and sent around the world like documents'." **page fifty five**

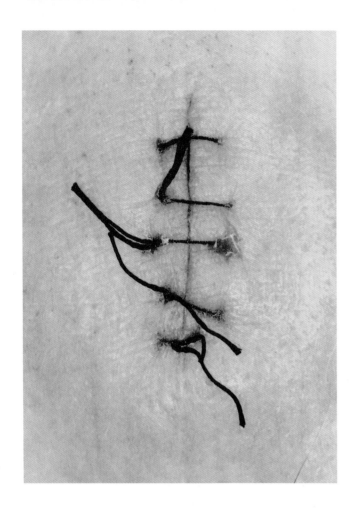

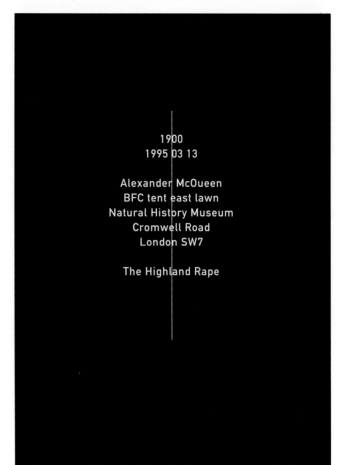

1900
1995 03 13

Alexander McQueen
BFC tent east lawn
Natural History Museum
Cromwell Road
London SW7

The Highland Rape

230004 002567   108
ALEXANDER MCQUEEN
M.A. COMMERCIALE S.R.L.
VIA LUIGI EINAUDI 160
CIVITANOVA M. [MC]
ITALIA

                                   B:1969

project show invite. **title the highland rape autumn/winter 1995. designers Angus Hyland,
Silvia Gaspardo Moro. client Alexander McQueen. photographer Nico Schwartz. image from the triptych installation memories of you 1994.
accompanying text** "the Scottish Highlands have been of great inspiration to many designers in the past. But they have been romanticised
all too often. There were swathes of tartan but only as a protection against the elements. Protection proved not to be enough against the
fury of soldiers, as in many places and at many times across the world." project logo. **designers Angus Hyland, Silvia Gaspardo Moro. client
Alexander McQueen. year 1995.** project tyre-track dress. **title birds spring/summer 1995. designer Alexander McQueen. page fifty seven**

YOHJI YAMAMOTO

PRODUCT CONTROL

100% QUALITY and
ABSOLUTE UNIFOMITY
INSURED

49
Lbs.
Net

FRESHNESS

UNSURPASSED

NO.
10031943

MANUFACTURED BY YOHJI YAMAMOTO INC.

THERE IS MORE
ACTION TO BE
DONE TO FIGHT
AIDS THAN TO
WEAR THIS
T·SHIRT BUT IT'S
A GOOD START

MADE IN ITALY

WARNING

TO AVOID ANY DANGER OF SUFFOCATION KEEP AWAY FROM BABIES AND CHILDREN
DO NOT USE IN CRIBS, BEDS, CARRIAGES OR PLAY PENS. THIS BAG IS NOT A TOY

project printed shirt. **title Yohji Yamamoto spring/summer 1993 catalogue. art director Hisao Sugiura. designers Toshio Matsuura, Yasunobu Kawajiri, Studio Super Compass. photographers Thierry Chomel, Yutaka Yamamoto. video cameraman Luc Riolon. text Yohji Yamamoto.** project AIDS t-shirt. **title Martin Margiela spring/summer 1995. stockists Browns. page fifty nine**

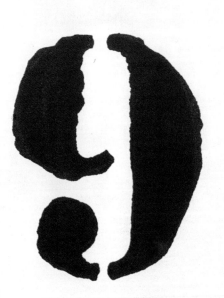

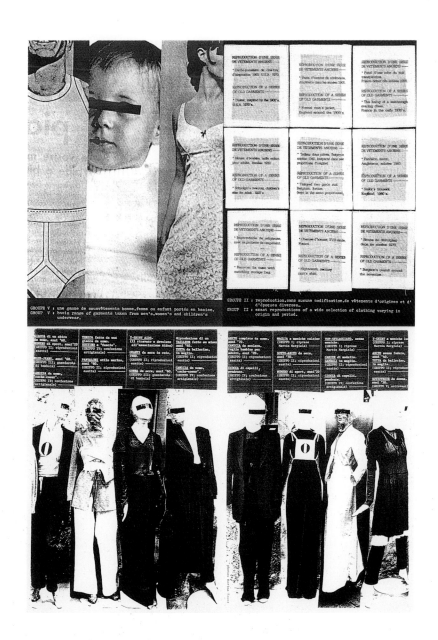

project bib. title Martin Margiela autumn/winter 1994. private collection Turin. project label. title Martin Margiela trade mark. project magazine article. title before and after fashion a project for *Artforum* by Martin Margiela March 1995. text Olivier Zahm "recycled style? Antifashion provocation? High fashion's answer to a grungy zeitgeist? These are a few of the dubious epithets that have greeted Martin Margiela's clothes since his debut spring/summer '89 collection. Add to them the promiscuous moniker *deconstruction* and it is plain that not only have Margiela's clothing designs disconcerted and shocked, they have also been misunderstood." page sixty one

VICTIMISATION. CREATING LABEL LOYALTY.
GRAPHIC DESIGNERS ADD THE ESSENTIAL
EXTRAS. FASHION ADDICTS COLLECT.

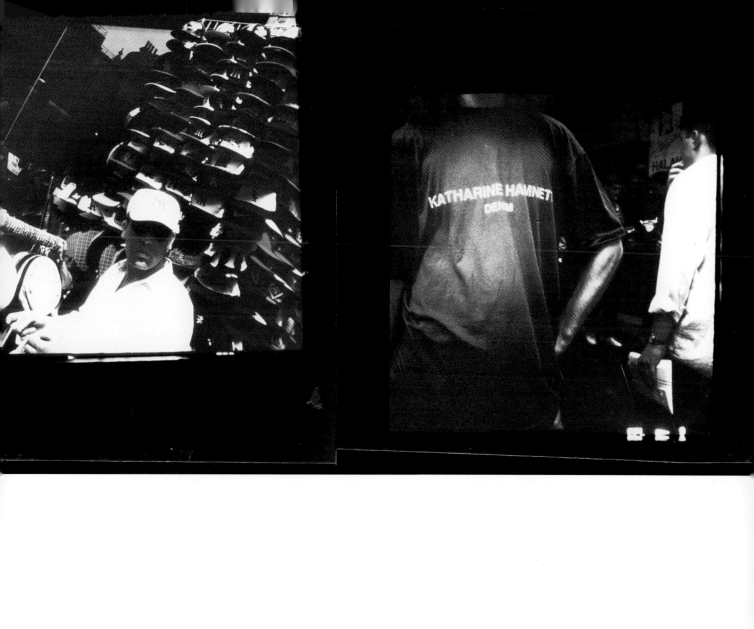

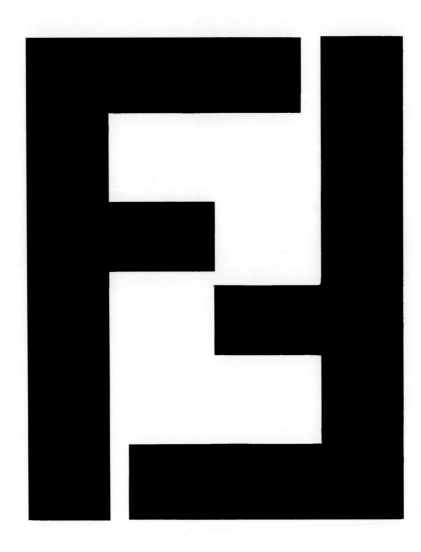

project logo. **title Fendi. design company**
Minale Tattersfield and Partners Limited. client Fendi. year 1993. project logo. **title JR cross logo with eagle. designer David Richmond.**
design company David Richmond Associates. client John Richmond. year 1993. illustrators David Richmond, Al Jones. page sixty seven

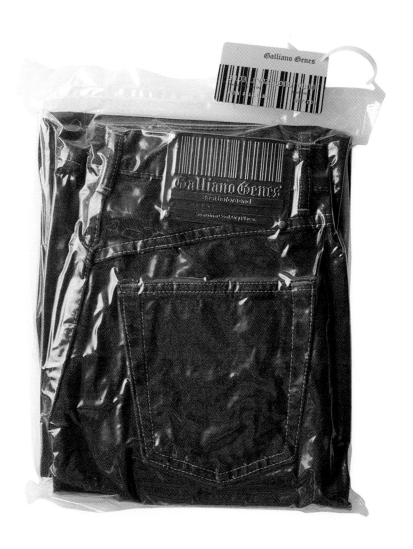

project show invites. **title John Galliano spring/summer 1991. designers Richard Smith, Cara Gallardo. design company Area. client John Galliano. typographer Richard Smith. quote Richard Smith** "all the stuff with John Galliano was always very vague. Initially he would run through the story behind the collection with us, his reference points. He used lots of union jacks in the collection which is why we used that image. It took a month including production, but we talked about it for six weeks, then mocked-up a washing line with plastic bags filled with mixed up colours and tested them. He was very keen to get the colours right, but the glitter made of glass punctured them and John liked the way they leaked all over these well-dressed women. He was very open to ideas, never wanted to tell you what to do. We worked with him for two years." **project product promotion/gift. title Galliano genes. designers Richard Smith, Cara Gallardo. design company Area. client John Galliano. year 1991. typographer Richard Smith. quote Richard Smith** "John Galliano tried to make some money doing jeans. This was a press pack sent out to fashion people and every editor had a personalised card with their date of birth and size. We tried to make it look like a credit card, and we packaged the jeans like a piece of meat. He said to us, 'I'm thinking of doing this', and we just extended the plastic idea, after the invite. When you do fashion work you get to know lots of weird processes and it comes in handy for other jobs." **page sixty nine**

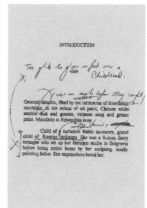

invite. **title John Galliano spring/summer 1991.** designers Richard Smith, Cara Gallardo. design company Area. client John Galliano.
illustrator Studio John Galliano. typographer Richard Smith. project show invite. **title John Galliano spring/summer 1995. page seventy one**

project catalogue. **title Koji Tatsuno. designers Richard Smith, Cara Gallardo. design company Area. art director/stylist Yvonne Sporre. client Koji Tatsuno. year 1990. photographers Anton Corbijn, Juergen Ostarhild. typographer Richard Smith. hair Joe Carney. make-up Lisa Butler. quote Richard Smith** "we spent weeks trying to find black elastic bands, Yvonne Sporre doesn't give in until it becomes really impossible. Yvonne liked the idea of many different papers and processes, like walking into a second hand shop and finding all these different things, it's like a collection, a source book and the best way to do that is in a loose leaf format, it's more economical. It all happened incredibly late for the deadline and we had to collate 500 catalogues, with material from three printers and the perspex. We took off the protective cover, hoovered the static, five people worked all night, they went to Italy next morning, and the courier nearly lost them. All Koji's catalogues were done before the show, like a taster, one of the reasons we used perspex was because he used glass in the show, we thought about using glass but it was too impractical. This was the first time Anton did any really amazing colour photography. He developed this special process, drawing with light in a dark room, the person has to stand still and you draw around them, and sometimes you get a lot of shadow." **project show invite. title Koji Tatsuno autumn/winter 1993. designers Richard Smith, Cara Gallardo. design company Area. art director/stylist Yvonne Sporre. client Koji Tatsuno. typographer Richard Smith. page seventy three**

title under the blue Koji Tatsuno. designers Richard Smith, Cara Gallardo. design company Area. art director/stylist Yvonne Sporre. client Koji Tatsuno. year 1993. typographer Richard Smith. quote Richard Smith "the invite was going to be rubber stamped and it didn't dry. It was onto floral paper used for wrapping flowers, because of all those floral print dresses at the time, and we thought simple, rubber stamp onto a bit of paper. The problem is Yvonne always wants something a little bit weird, like she wanted orange ink and so we had to get paint or lino ink, and we sat there one Sunday waiting for it all to dry." project show invite. **title ladies like gentlemen. designers Richard Smith, Cara Gallardo. design company Area. art director/stylist Yvonne Sporre. client Koji Tatsuno. year 1992. typographer Richard Smith. quote Richard Smith** "where do you buy 1,500 paper doilies and can you do your own design? Someone said, 'go to this Jewish deli in Golders Green', and that's where we got them. Then we printed them letter press thanks to a very flexible printer." **page seventy five**

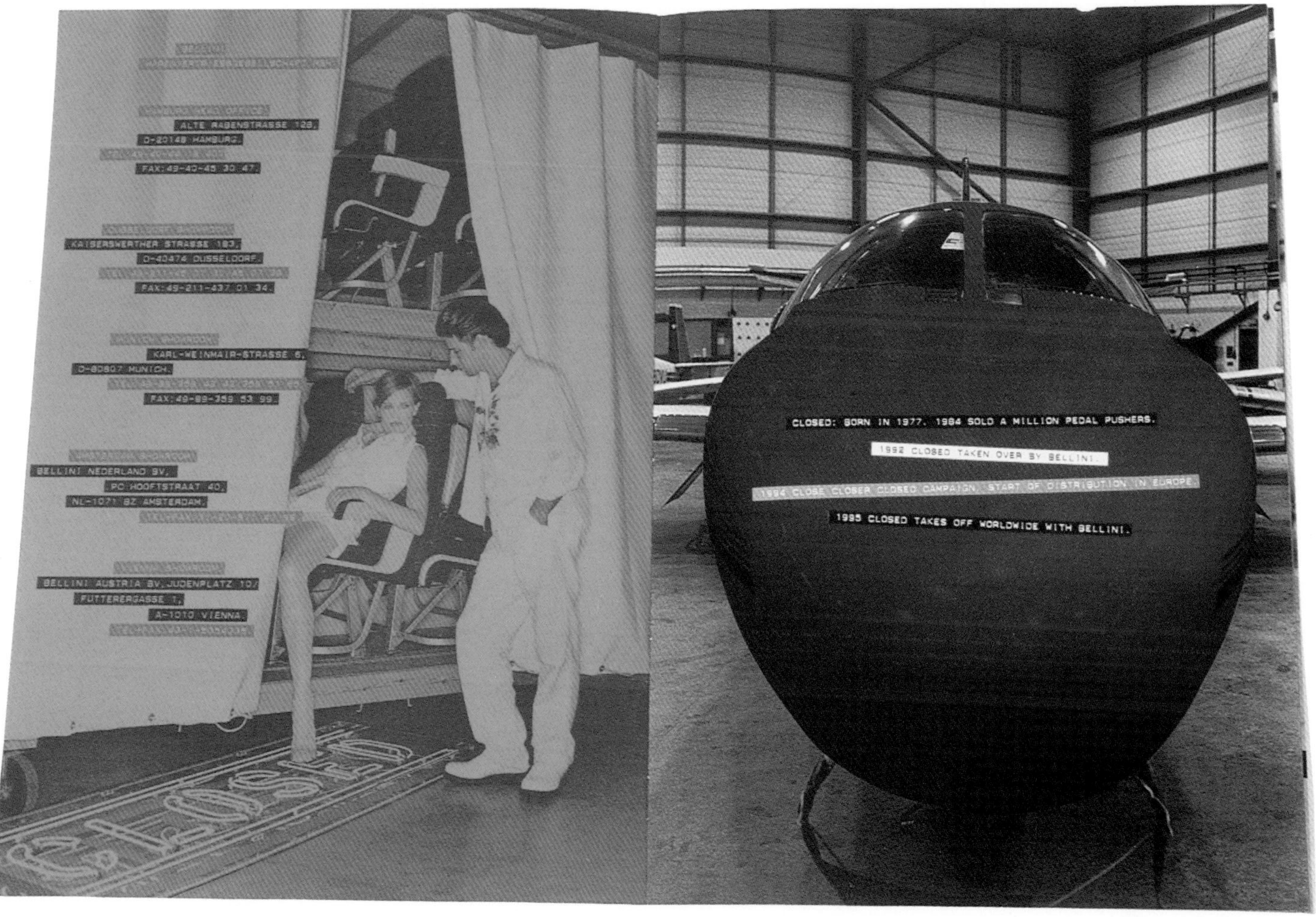
ALTE RABENSTRASSE 123,
D-20148 HAMBURG.
FAX:49-40-45 30 47.
KAISERSWERTHER STRASSE 183,
D-40474 DUSSELDORF.
FAX:49-211-437 01 34.
KARL-WEINMAIR-STRASSE 6,
D-80807 MUNICH.
FAX:49-89-359 53 99.
BELLINI NEDERLAND BV,
PC HOOFTSTRAAT 40,
NL-1071 BZ AMSTERDAM.
BELLINI AUSTRIA BV,JUDENPLATZ 10/
FUTTERERGASSE 1,
A-1010 VIENNA.
CLOSED: BORN IN 1977. 1984 SOLD A MILLION PEDAL PUSHERS.
1992 CLOSED TAKEN OVER BY BELLINI.
1994 CLOSE CLOSER CLOSED CAMPAIGN. START OF DISTRIBUTION IN EUROPE.
1995 CLOSED TAKES OFF WORLDWIDE WITH BELLINI.

project catalogue. **title closed. designer Richard Smith. design company Area. art director/stylist Yvonne Sporre. client Bellini Gmbh. year 1995. photographer Peter Jacob. typographer Richard Smith. hair Colin Roy at Streeters. make-up Lisa Butler at Marina Jones. comment** "Area and Yvonne Sporre continue their collaboration working for Closed, a jeanswear company, after earning their reputation with Koji Tatsuno, the most esoteric of designers – another example of the mainstream learning from the avant-garde." **page seventy seven**

KATHARINE HAMNETT
LONDON

KATHARINE HAMNETT

project woven label. **title Katharine Hamnett London.** project double-page print ad. **title Katharine Hamnett autumn/winter 1984. photographer Peter Lindbergh. quote Julian Vogel, Modus Publicity** "Katharine Hamnett oversees everything that has her name on it. As far as models and photographers go Katharine has a huge input. She has a reputation for using people early on in their careers and catapulting them forward - Juergen Teller, Ellen Von Unwerth, with Terry Richardson being the latest." **page seventy nine**

KATHARINE HAMNETT

PHOTO: JUERGEN TELLER

GFT (GB) LTD

**KATHARINE HAMNETT
DENIM**

project catalogue. title Katharine Hamnett the movie autumn/winter 1991. photographer Ellen Von Unwerth. model Naomi Campbell. project double-page print ad. title Katharine Hamnett spring/summer 1993. photographer Ellen Von Unwerth. project print ad. title Katharine Hamnett Denim spring/summer 1994. photographer Juergen Teller. page eighty one

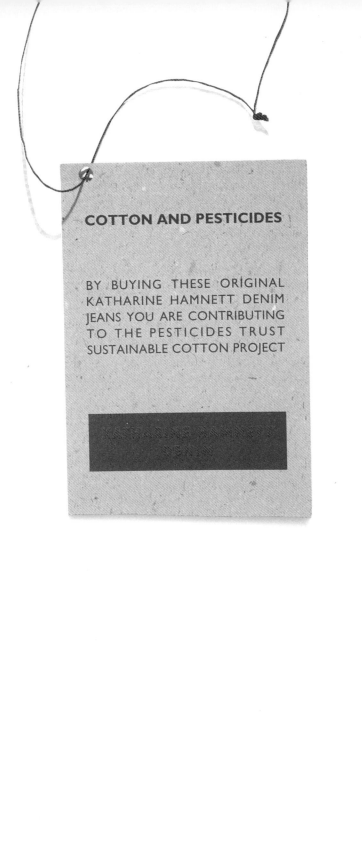

COTTON AND PESTICIDES

BY BUYING THESE ORIGINAL
KATHARINE HAMNETT DENIM
JEANS YOU ARE CONTRIBUTING
TO THE PESTICIDES TRUST
SUSTAINABLE COTTON PROJECT

CHIC

OOO-L'AH-L'AH
PARIS

CLEAN UP OR DIE

WORLD PEACE NOW

project swing tag. **title cotton and pesticides Katharine Hamnett Denim. designer in-house. year 1994.** project Katharine Hamnett show invites. **title chic spring/summer 1987. title ooo-l'ah-l'ah spring/summer 1990. title spring/summer 1994. title clean up or die autumn/winter 1989. title world peace now spring/summer 1988. title menswear spring/summer 1989. designer in-house.** project double-page spread. **title opera house Hamburg 1988 from** *Wolfgang Tillmans.* **year 1995. photographer Wolfgang Tillmans. editor Burkhard Riemshneider. publisher Taschen. page eighty three**

project Press Association
photograph. **title designer with message for Margaret. year 1984. text on reverse of photograph** "premier Margaret Thatcher wears a full-length black velvet gown and black and white blouse at No 10 Downing Street, London, where she hosted tonight's reception for British Fashion Week designers. In this picture she greets designer Katharine Hamnett whose offbeat outfit is emblazoned with a missile protest message." **project logo ideas for diffusion line. designers/typographers Tom Hingston, Paul Allen. client Katharine Hamnett. year 1995.**

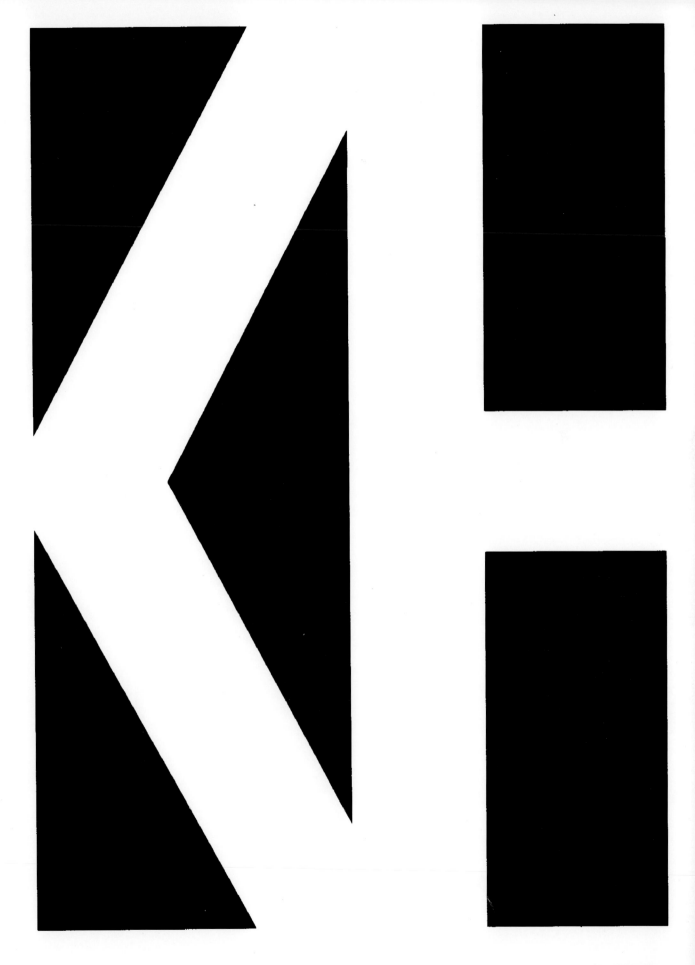

project catalogue. designers Tom Bonauro, John Choe. design company Tom Bonauro Design. client Yang.
year 1994. photographer Stephano Massei. models Rebecca "DJ Polywog" Corbett, Brandon Gartland. project new year's announcement.
title whole lotta love. designers Tom Bonauro, Jamie Oliveri. design company Tom Bonauro Design. client Mac. year 1993. page eighty seven

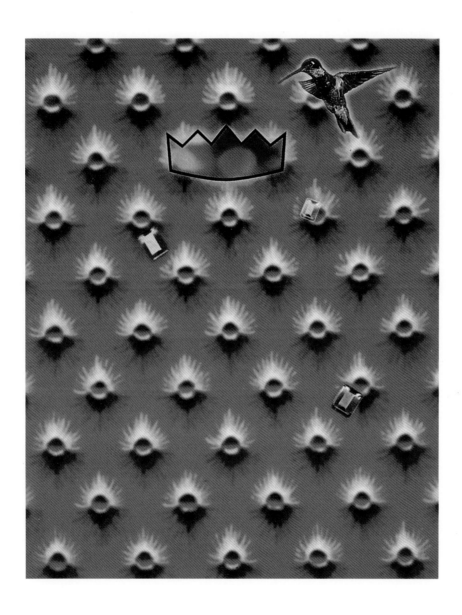

project catalogue. title Diana Slavin fall/winter 1993. designer Tom Bonauro. design company Tom Bonauro Design. client Diana Slavin. photographer Jeffery Newbury. hair/make-up Edie Valentine. project catalogue. title Diana Slavin fall/winter 1994. designers Tom Bonauro, John Choe. design company Tom Bonauro Design. client Diana Slavin. photographer Jeffery Newbury. hair/make-up Edie Valentine. project shop card. designer Tom Bonauro, Jamie Oliveri. design company Tom Bonauro Design. client Todd Oldham. year 1993. page eighty nine

project shop installation. title *The Face*/Comme des Garçons. art director Lee Swillingham. design company *The Face*. client Comme des Garçons. year 1995. photographer Schoerner. stylist Adam Howe. hair Jimo Solako. make-up Cathy Lomax. comment "the Tokyo flag-ship store of Comme des Garçons has become a site for photographic installations which defy the interior/exterior divide and play with scale. The first installation, by renowned New York artist Cindy Sherman, of her manipulative self-portraits has been superseded by Swillingham and Schoerner's hyper-real suburban catwalk shot in London." page ninety one

HYPER

HYPER

HYPER

HYPER

project press ads. title Hyper Hyper.
designers Sammy Farrington, Clifford Hiscock. design company Farrington Associates. client Hyper Hyper. year 1993. photographer Zanna.
typographer Sammy Farrington. project instore photo-frieze. title DUK 94/95. art directors Jane Alexander, Tim Hopgood. design company
Dart Partnership. client Dolcis. photographer Peter Anderson. stylist Cathy Dixon. hair/make-up Jackie Hamilton Smith. page ninety three

Issey Miyake spring/summer 1993. project invite. title Issey Miyake christmas party. designers Anthony Michael, Stephanie Nash. design company Michael Nash Associates. client Issey Miyake UK Limited. year 1991. project carrier bag. title Issey Miyake cotton label. designers Anthony Michael, Stephanie Nash. design company Michael Nash Associates. client Issey Miyake UK Limited. year 1995. page ninety five

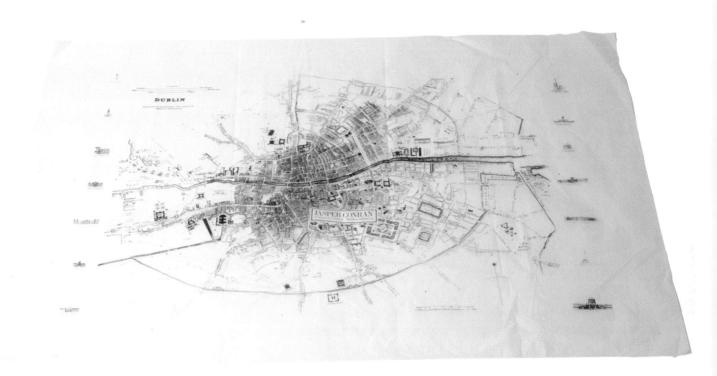

title Jasper Conran autumn/winter 1988. designers Stephanie Nash, Anthony Michael. design company Michael Nash Associates. client Jasper Conran Limited. photographer Peter Lindbergh. hair Julien D'Is. make-up Stephane Marais. quote Stephanie Nash "Jasper Conran, his career was on the up and up and he was one of the first designers to think about graphics and what graphics can do. He found us through seeing a letter head we'd designed for a record company and the owner's girlfriend worked for him. At the beginning he gave me very specific instructions, but now it's shorthand. He might give me a source, an architect, a bit of fabric, something that is an inspiration for each collection.

I do the show material, invites, programmes, packaging, every single label, everything since 1986. I think Jasper Conran has got the most amazing colour sense, it's what I like most about what he does and I personally am influenced by his colour use. I really look at the clothes, and the texture, but really his thing is colour, he'll do a green coat and line it in lilac. Each season the show material comes first, then after the show we think about photography and the catalogue. It's a collaboration, sometimes he styles it, sometimes he'll bring someone in, or use someone who's working for him. He'd have a very strong view about the photography, but again it would be project oriented.

When we used Peter Lindbergh Jasper Conran very much had Lartigue in mind and that Lartigue woman in his head, so it was finding a contemporary photographer to do that and Peter fitted the bill. The photographer will initially do a picture selection, then we'll all sift through them. This was the one we spent the most time and money on and the images were put in like art plates, this was the one where we had the most control. It was a good collection to work with, it went with what we were trying to do and we had enough money to spend to do it, everyone got on." **project tissue paper from retail packaging range. title Dublin. designers Stephanie Nash, Anthony Michael. design company Michael Nash Associates. client Jasper Conran Limited. year 1987. quote Stephanie Nash** "Jasper's brief to me was, 'Watch those old Hollywood movies for when those women come back with all those boxes piled high and tied with ribbons.' That was very much what we were trying to do with the Jasper Conran packaging, it was my idea to do an old map of each city, where the shops were, to wrap the clothes." **page ninety seven**

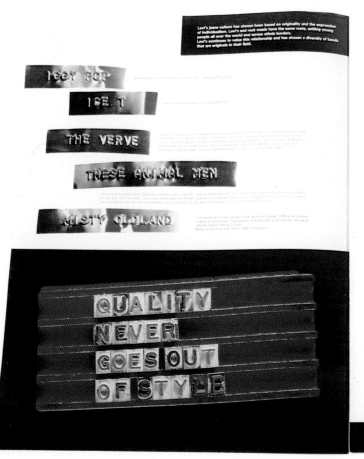

QUALITY NEVER GOES OUT OF STYLE

project point of sale cut-outs. title heroes, Ice T and Iggy Pop. designers/typographers Stephen Male, Neil Edwards. design company Nice. client Levi Strauss Scandinavia. year 1994. photographer David Sims. project catalogue. title the heroes issue. designers/typographers Stephen Male, Neil Edwards. design company Nice. client Levi Strauss Scandinavia. year 1994. photographer David Sims. page ninety nine

regular

project catalogue. title cape cod. designers/typographers Stephen Male, Neil Edwards, Richard Bonner-Morgan. design company Nice. client Levi Strauss UK Limited. year 1992. photographer Donald Christie. stylist Simon Foxton. project point of sale. title loose. designers Stephen Male, Richard Bonner-Morgan. typographer Neil Edwards. design company Nice. client Levi Strauss UK Limited. year 1994. photographer Craig McDean. project point of sale. title red tab fit communication. designers Peter Miles, Damon Murray, Stephen Sorrell. design company Fuel. client Levi Strauss UK Limited. year 1995. photographer Matthew Donaldson. stylist Simon Foxton. page one hundred and one

present times

From chaos and danger...opportunity.

Helen Storey Autumn/Winter 1991 Collection

project show programme. **title present times Helen Storey autumn/winter 1991. designer Moira Bogue. design company Bogue & Hopgood. client Helen Storey. illustrator Helen Storey's son. typographer Moira Bogue.** project product catalogue. **designers Richard Smith, Cara Gallardo. design company Area. client Jacqueline Rabun. year 1994. photographer Mark Mattock. typographer Richard Smith. quote Richard Smith** "we always do very natural looking things for Jacqueline. She uses leather, the jewellery comes in leather pouches, so we use brown and silver foil blocking. She had lots of pictures and wanted something up-datable, we talked about xeroxing, that's how they did it before, but we used low-resolution scans. She likes things to have a rough edge, she doesn't like things to be super highly polished. It's very rough and ready but looks right, so the technology is right for it. **page one hundred and three**

Geoffrey Beene

y

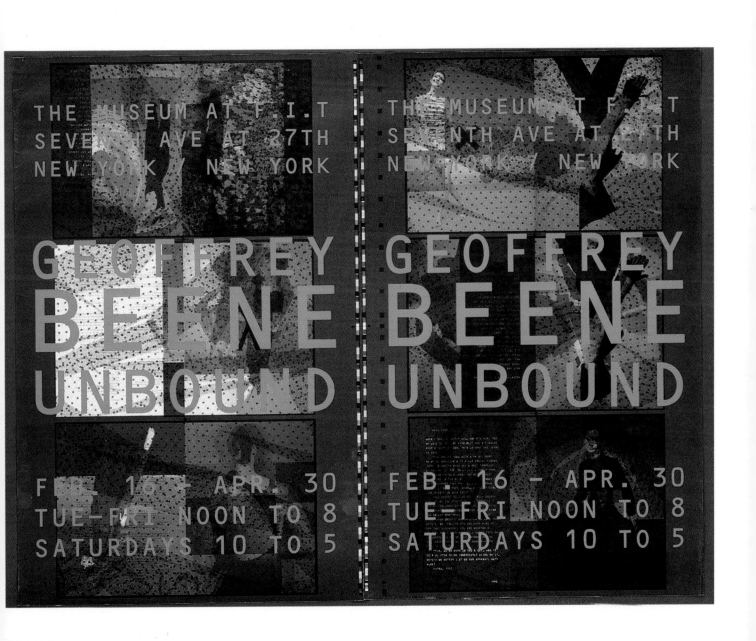

project book cover. title Geoffrey Beene. designer/typographer J Abbott Miller. design company Design/Writing/Research. client Harry N Abrams Inc Publishers. year 1995. photographer Andrew Eccles. project exhibition catalogue. designer J Abbot Miller. design company Design/Writing/Research. client Geoffrey Beene. year 1993. photographer Hiro. project poster. title Geoffrey Beene unbound. designer/typographer J Abbott Miller. design company Design/Writing/Research. client Geoffrey Beene, Fashion Institute of Technology New York. year 1993. text "the poster was made from the printer's make-ready sheets, from the exhibition catalogue. Each poster was unique as the type was silk-screened on top." page one hundred and five

project show programme. **title Phillip Treacy show.** designers Anthony Michael, Stephanie Nash. design company Michael Nash Associates. client Phillip Treacy. year 1994. project retail packaging. **title Egg.** designers Anthony Michael, Stephanie Nash, Teresa Roviras. design company Michael Nash Associates. client Egg. year 1993. quote Stephanie Nash "I think we work with very strong, creative people a lot of the time. Everything we do is to try and get inside the client's head, to know what she wants, what she's trying to do. So I just put together some textures, from what she explained to me and, again, think outside of why it has to be a carrier bag, it doesn't have to be. I did some ideas using a sack and calico and maybe a paper envelope. The paper is rag paper made from the off-cuts of the cotton clothes in the designer, Ashe's, workshop in India, and they sew them on their machines. They vary a bit, we just did a drawing, faxed it to India and they sent them back." **page one hundred and seven**

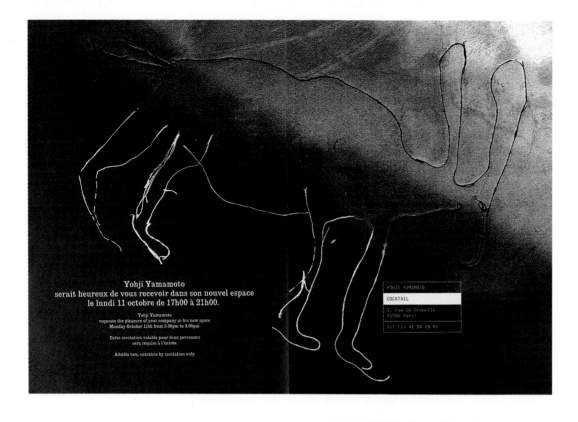

Yohji Yamamoto
serait heureux de vous recevoir dans son nouvel espace
le lundi 11 octobre de 17h00 à 21h00.

Yohji Yamamoto
requests the pleasure of your company in his new space
Monday October 11th from 5:00pm to 9:00pm.

Cette invitation valable pour deux personnes
sera requise à l'entrée.

Admits two, entrance by invitation only.

YOHJI YAMAMOTO

COCKTAIL

3, rue de Grenelle
75006 Paris

Tel (1) 42 84 28 87

Y's for men
YOHJI YAMAMOTO

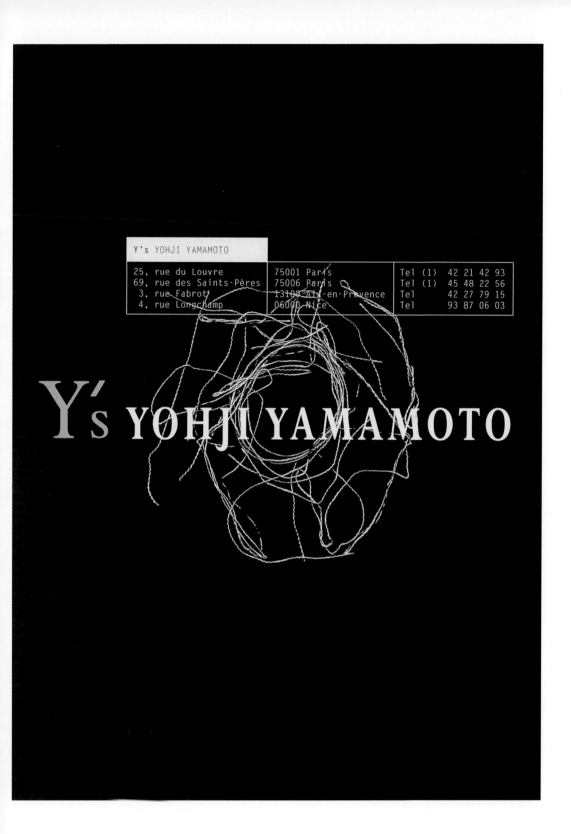

Y's YOHJI YAMAMOTO

25. rue du Louvre	75001 Paris	Tel (1) 42 21 42 93
69. rue des Saints-Pères	75006 Paris	Tel (1) 45 48 22 56
3. rue Fabrot	13100 Aix-en-Provence	Tel 42 27 79 15
4. rue Longchamp	06000 Nice	Tel 93 87 06 03

project shop opening invite. **title Y's. design company/illustrators M/M. client Yohji Yamamoto. year 1994.** project series of press ads announcing new line. **title Y's. design company/illustrators M/M. client Yohji Yamamoto. year 1994. photographer Ferdinando Scianna @Magnum. hair/make-up Marc Lopez. page one hundred and nine**

Y

m

Autumn/Winter 93/94

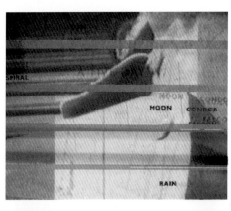

project catalogue and postcards. **title Y's for men autumn/winter 1993. designer Takeiciro Morinaga. design company Art et Métier Co Limited. client Y's for men Yohji Yamamoto Co Limited. year 1993.** project 55 second commercial for menswear designer. **title John Tate. designer Louise Lattimore. client John Tate. year 1995.** page one hundred and eleven

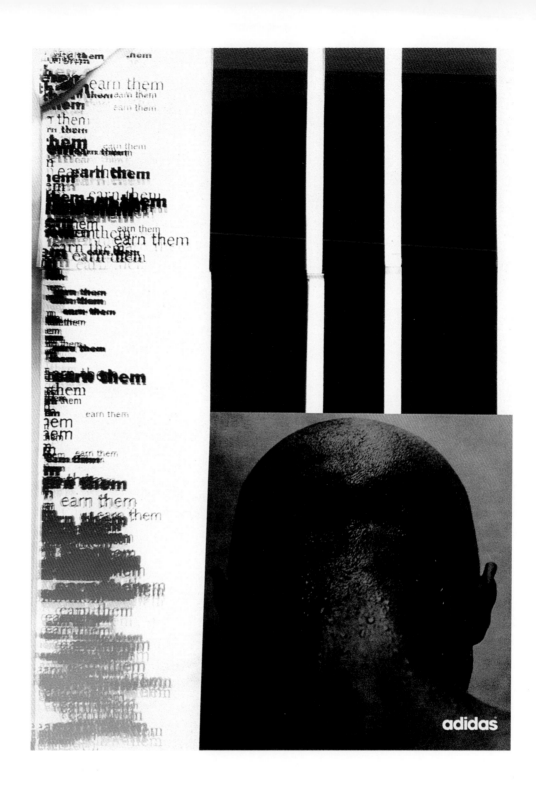

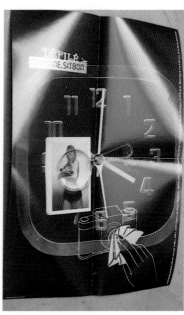

project display boxes. **designers James Hodgson, Gareth Davies. design company in-house. client Easy Jeans. year 1994.** project press pack, promotional broadsheet. **title Griffin Laundry, surfing the digital highway for autumn/winter 1995 and beyond. designers Jeff Griffin, Mervyn Rands. design company Penrose Design Limited. client Jeff Griffin, Griffin Laundry. year 1995. photographer Mike Diver at Nick Selby. typographer Mervyn Rands. stylists Jason Kelvin, Gavin Fernandez. assistant James Sleaford. hair Adam Bryant at Streeters. make-up Sharon Dowsett at Premier Plus. comment** "Jeff Griffin's post-apocalyptic, high-tech workwear is sold through the Griffin Laundry home-page on the internet." **page one hundred and seventeen**

CABOURN®

Nigel Cabourn Ltd 6/7 Chimney Mill, Claremont Road, Newcastle Upon Tyne NE2 4AL. Tel: 091 232 3772. Fax: 091 232 6774
Sales and UK Agent David Barnett, 40 Floral Street, London WC2 E9DG. Tel: 071 240 0845. Fax: 071 379 4659
Japanese Licensee Kazu Tomeoka, Anglobal Ltd, Nishi Azabu 8 Building, Minato Ku, Nishi Azabu S–11–S, Tokyo. Tel: 813 34981391. Fax: 813 34064536

title Nigel Cabourn autumn/winter 1994. designers/typographers/stylists Paul Neale, Andrew Stevens. design company Graphic Thought Facility. client Nigel Cabourn. year 1994. illustrator Alan Baker. project promotional literature. title Wallace Sewell identity. designers Paul Neale, Andrew Stevens. design company Graphic Thought Facility. client Wallace Sewell. year 1993. page one hundred and nineteen

ROMEO GIGLI

Milano - C.so Como 10
Milano - C.so Venezia 11
Parigi - 46 Rue de Sevigne
New York - 21 East 68th Street

ROMEO GIGLI

JOHN CALE

JOHN CALE MUSIC INC.
4 Greenwich Mews,
New York, New York, 10014-6304
212.807.6479 - FX 366.5056.
12/21/94

John Cale's latest work is centred around Live Music & Speech
Performances with the Classic Films - 'The Unknown' by Tod Browning
and 'Eat' and 'Kiss' by Andy Warhol.

project newspaper ad. title legs. designer Claudio Dell'Olio. design company Box, Milan. client Romeo Gigli Menswear. year 1990. photographer Dennis Oppenheim. project press ad. title blur. designer Claudio Dell'Olio. design company Box, Milan. client Romeo Gigli. year 1990. photographer Ilvio Gallo. project catalogue. title Romeo Gigli Menswear spring/summer 1995. designer Christopher Radl. client Romeo Gigli Menswear. photographers Max Vadukul, Maria Vittoria Corradi Backhaus. stylist Nicoletta Santoro. comment "Romeo Gigli's Menswear catalogue appeals to an audience whose heroes are rock stars of a certain generation." page one hundred and twenty one

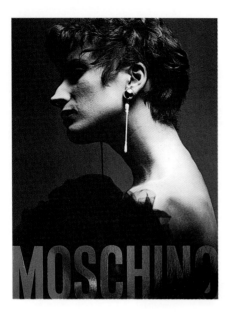

MOSCHINO

anarchy

bon chic,
bon genre

classico

moschino

A + + + =

B

C

M ?

project book. title Moschino. designer Daniele Basilico. design
company Box, Milan. client Moschino. year 1988. photographer Fabrizio Ferri. stylist Franco Moschino. page one hundred and twenty three

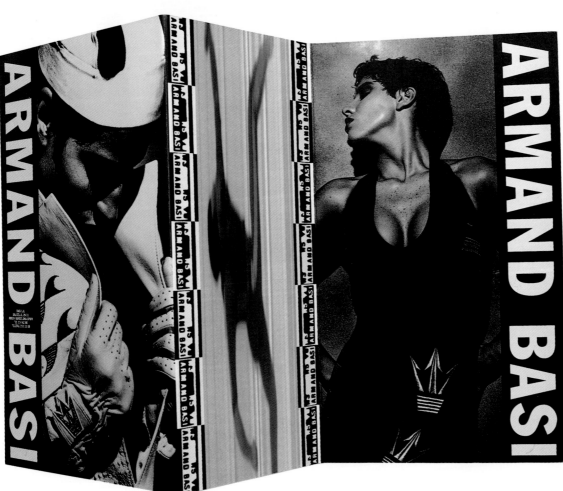

title fire. art director/typographer/stylist Robin Derrick. design company Box. client Armand Basi. year 1992. photographer Norman Watson. project window display. title super heroes. art director/typographer Robin Derrick. design company Box. client Armand Basi. year 1991. photographer Norman Watson. stylist David Bradshaw. project catalogue. title Anna Molinari. designer Claudio Dell'Olio. design company Box, Milan. client Blumarine. year 1994. photographer Helmut Newton. page one hundred and twenty five

DOLCE & GABBANA

SHEILYN CENN
FOTOGRAFATA DA STEVEN MEISEL

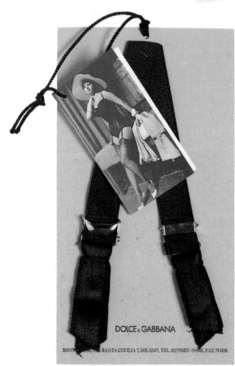

DOLCE & GABBANA

SHOWROOM VIA SANTA CECILIA 7, MILANO, TEL. 02/79085-79085, FAX 784436

project catalogue. title Sherilyn Fenn. designer Claudio Dell'Olio. design company Box, Milan. client Dolce & Gabbana. year 1991. photographer Steven Meisel. project show invite. title Sofia Loren. designer Claudio Dell'Olio. design company Box, Milan. client Dolce & Gabbana. year 1991. project double-page press ad. title Isabella Rossellini. designer Claudio Dell'Olio. design company Box, Milan. client Dolce & Gabbana. year 1989. photographer Steven Meisel. page one hundred and twenty seven

manifest ones shoe

project underwear

packaging. **title Gef. design company/photographer/illustrator April Greiman. client Gef, Maria Echavarria. year 1991.** project transparent

poster. **title manifest ones shoe. design company/typographers/stylists 10x5. client Steadman. year 1993. one hundred and twenty nine**

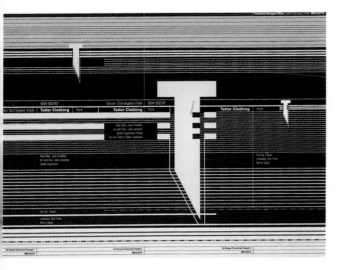

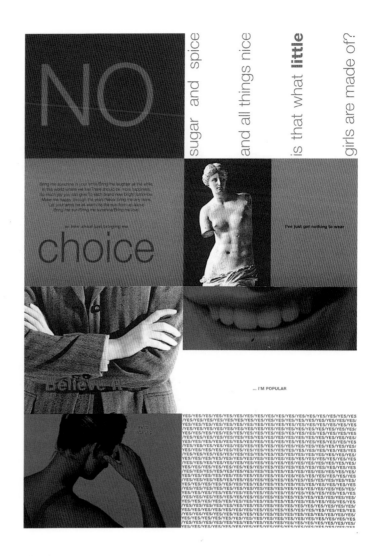

project window installation. **title Picasso's women.**
designers Sara Safiullah, Godfried Donkor. design company P.art One Inc. client Harvey Nichols. year 1994. project window installation. **title
to be the best. designer Rana Salam. client Harvey Nichols. year 1994. illustrator billboard artist working in the Lebanon.** project
promotional flyer. **title Tatler Clothing. designer/typographer Chris Ashworth. design company Orange. client Tatler Clothing. year 1992.**
project postcards. **title Principles Petite. design company The Trigger Foundation. client Principles. year 1994.** page one hundred and thirty one

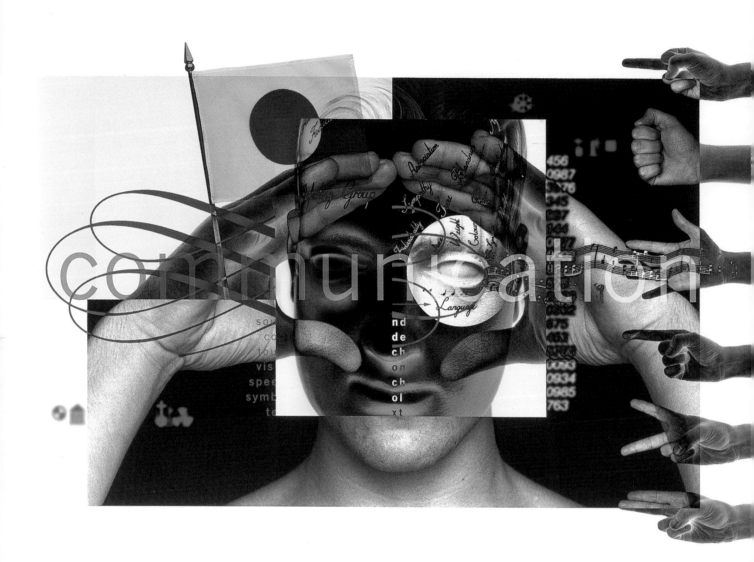

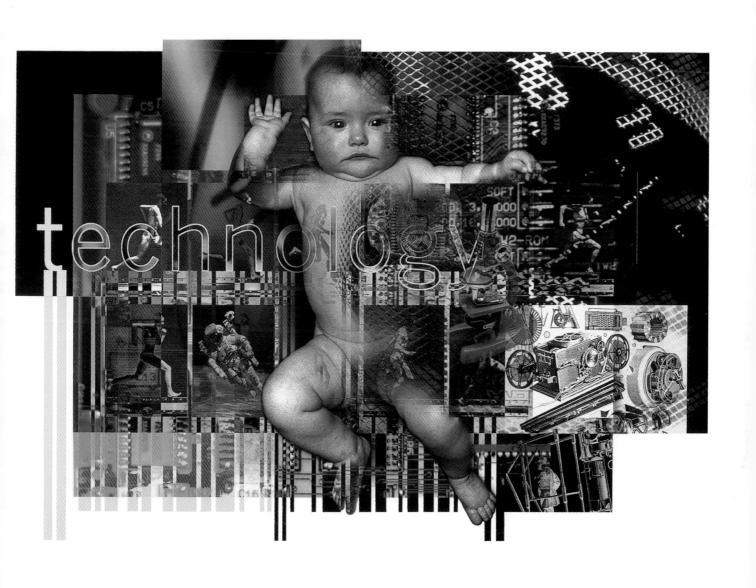

**project audio-visual installation. title
Kobe Fashion Museum. designers Andy Altmann, David Ellis, Patrick Morrissey. design company Why Not Associates. client Dai Nippon
Printing. year 1995. photographers Rocco Redondo, PhotoDisc Image Library. comment** "an audio-visual installation made up of thousands of
images programmed to layer over and merge into each other will be projected around the four walls of the entrance hall in the as yet to be
completed fashion museum. The Why Not Associates' inaugural installation will be seen by the public in 1997." **page one hundred and thirty three**

YOU CAN TAKE YOUR DREAM BACK HOME. IMAGE CREATION MANIPULATION MEDIATION. BETWEEN FASHION AND ITS PUBLIC STANDS THE ART DIRECTOR. THE POWER AND ILLUSION OF THE MEDIA

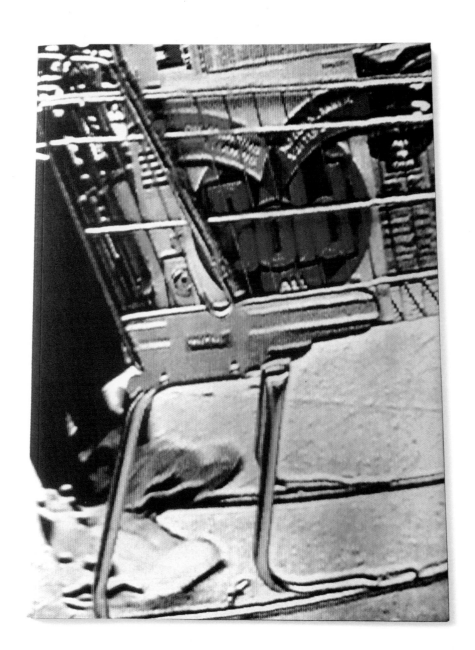

Go 1992. design company Pentagram. art director Peter Saville. client Yohji Yamamoto. photographers Nina Schultz, Trevor Key, Norbert Schoerner, Donald Christie. stylist Melanie Ward. hair Willie at Willie Smart's. make-up Dick Page. quote Peter Saville "the women's collection was brilliant, Yohji sent everything out down the runway with Nike trainers and it reminded me of an American woman I'd seen in Europa in Notting Hill one night, in a blue raincoat and trainers. It was that New York street look done well, it was a great collection, so I didn't mind showing the clothes. We just went out and did what we wanted. Nina got Melanie Ward to do her first big commercial job. All the people who a year later became the megastars, hair, make-up, this kind of London clique. It was the most stressful month of my life. I tried to art direct it. Nina and I worked out locations. When I look back on this catalogue now I see it was everybody's input. We shot clothes on 35 mm and video and we went back to Europa, where I'd seen the women. We went under the Westway. We did still-life stuff with Trevor Key. The cover was the supermarket trolley. The whole feeling was spring in Manhattan, artists on the street. We went to Brixton gave the clothes to skateboarders and Nina videoed them, which was fun. Then I took the skateboard and Trevor shot it. We used Bruce Maclean for the men's stuff and let him do stuff in the studio, he put on three jackets, doing a bit of a funny performance. I tried a bit of photo-realism with Trevor, we spent a night trying to make a paint tube look like a photo-realist painting. Bruce did some painting and I got Donald Christie to take his picture with his painting shoes on. One men's jacket had holes burnt in it, so Trevor Key shot it on the light box to try and reburn the holes with the light. It was a bit *Paris Texas*, a bit *My Own Private Idaho* with a kind of road movie feeling. Yohji loved it, he said, 'Peter, silk dress £2,000, you give to a girl for basketball, I like it'. The customers didn't, because anybody who can afford a £2,000 dress can't relate to a black girl in Spike Lee glasses playing basketball. Because of this we did the Mr Koons basketball double-page spread. I said to Trevor Key 'just float it in white space and we'll carry on the art joke'." **page one hundred and thirty seven**

JIL SANDER

project slide box containing E-Z Go. project double-page press ad. **title Jil Sander spring/summer 1992. designer Peter Saville. art director Marc Ascoli. client Jil Sander. photographer Nick Knight. model Tatiana Patiz. quote Peter Saville** "the approach that Marc Ascoli and Nick Knight developed for Yohji, they went on to apply to Jil Sander". **page one hundred and thirty nine**

project catalogue. **title Jil Sander fall/winter 1992. designers Stephanie Nash, Anthony Michael. design company Michael Nash Associates. art director Marc Ascoli. client Jil Sander. photographer Nick Knight. hair Didier Malige at Frederic Fekkai. make-up Linda Cantello. model Christy Turlington. quote Stephanie Nash** "Marc was the art director, they went and did the pictures, came here and laid all the pictures out on the floor and we just did it. It was a very different way of working because there's no fashion designer, Marc becomes it, and he's quite commercial, he's got a kind of, 'I need three suit shots, I need a sunglasses shot, I need soft tailoring' approach. I briefed Nick, and then he would disagree with Marc and have an argument in French so I wouldn't understand what they were saying, but in the end it was OK. We came up with the format. We saw the pictures and we saw all the old catalogues that Peter Saville had done and noticed they all looked great as ads but when you went through them Nick's pictures didn't work together." **quote Anthony Michael** "before Nick started printing, we said 'we want the prints all to have the same tonal value and there's this rich aubergine, purple, brown and black, that was our input, and the colour and texture of this paper, the format and the running order." project catalogue. **title Jil Sander spring/summer 1995. design company M/M. art director Marc Ascoli. client Jil Sander. photographer Craig McDean. hair Eugene. make-up Pat McGrath. model Shalom.** project catalogue. **Jil Sander fall/winter 1994. design company M/M. art director Marc Ascoli. client Jil Sander. photographer Peter Lindbergh. hair Odile Gilbert. make-up Stéphane Marais. model Linda Evangelista. quote Caroline Roux** *Blueprint* **April 1995** "always there is a fluidity and sense of movement in the photography which, you can't help but surmise, comes directly from the elegant, comfortable clothes." **page one hundred and forty one**

project catalogue, advertising

images. **title Lundy Paul Smith spring/summer 1991. designer/typographer Alan K Aboud. design company Aboud Sodano. client Paul Smith Limited. photographer Hugh Hales-Tooke. stylists Patricia Keating, Håkan Rosenius. hair Peter Smith. quote Alan K Aboud** "the first thing we do each season is that I have a chat with Paul as to what the theme is for the collection and then we do the invitations although the collection's not finished at that stage. The themes are not that abstract, they take their lead from photographers or films or eras. He never really gave specific titles to collections until about three or four seasons ago mainly at the insistence of the Japanese because they really need something to explain to their customers, and I think when he started doing that it did fall into place a lot easier for me. You can see the way the catalogues started to come together much easier. We treat the year as one thing, so that from season to season the catalogues don't jump ridiculously in their style, and also now we use one photographer and the style has been set." **page one hundred and forty three**

Relaxing after a night in Swinging London

project catalogue, advertising images. **title London Paul Smith spring/summer 1992. art director/typographer Alan K Aboud. design company Aboud Sodano. client Paul Smith Limited. photographer Hugh Hales-Tooke. stylists Patricia Keating, Håkan Rosenius. hair Peter Smith.**

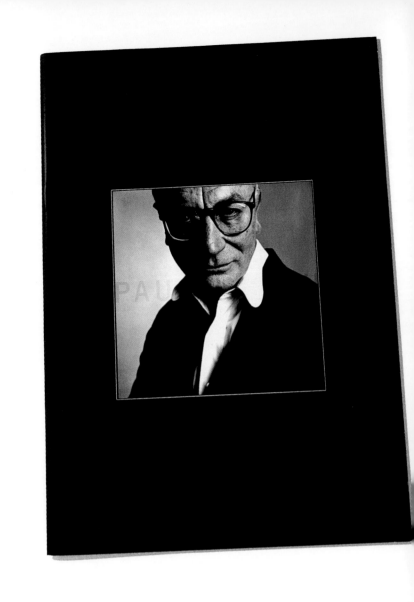

project catalogue, advertising images. **title 20th century mashers Paul Smith spring/summer 1994. art director/typographer Alan K Aboud. design company Aboud Sodano. client Paul Smith Limited. photographer David Bailey. stylists Patricia Keating, Håkan Rosenius. hair Peter Smith. quote Alan K Aboud** "originally we chose him because the season had a 1960s swinging London feel and the ideal person was David Bailey. From before I started, Paul had been using real people as opposed to models. It was a progression, we had to widen the net because we were using up our friends. So we don't use a casting agency, they're all contacts, whether it be from work or whatever way, if they're interesting enough they don't have to be attractive or young or old or fat or thin or whatever. It's nice to get a collection of people just to document, because the company has reached the level of recognition that we don't have to sell a product in the ad, we're selling the name which is great, but luckily we held out for long enough so that it was a natural progression, we've kind of evolved, there was a rationale behind it. Now clothes are secondary." project launch catalogue. **title Paul Smith Women spring/summer 1995. art director/typographer Alan K Aboud. design company Aboud Sodano. client Paul Smith Limited. photographer Julian Broad. stylist Håkan Rosenius. hair Val Garland. quote Alan K Aboud** "very occasionally, when it's kind of crucial that Paul needs to be at the shoot he'll be there, like the very first women's shoots he was there, because he wanted to make sure that what he was going to get was what he was looking for." **page one hundred and forty seven**

Paul Smith
BAG

YOSHINAGA CORPORATION
ヨシナガ株式会社
1-4-4, Yanagibashi, Taito-ku, Tokyo 111
Telephone: 03-3864-3961

image. **title Paul Smith toiletries. designer/typographer Alan K Aboud. design company Aboud Sodano. client Paul Smith Limited. year 1994. photographer/stylist Sandro Sodano.** project advertising image, part of a series of three. **title Paul Smith bag autumn/ winter 1994. designer/typographer Alan K Aboud. design company Aboud Sodano. client Paul Smith Limited. photographer/stylist Sandro Sodano. quote Alan K Aboud** "the way we do all the other lines, they're much more fashionable and very much more seasonal because we're product selling, not image selling." project gift catalogue. **title Paul Smith christmas 1990. designer/typographer Alan K Aboud. design company Aboud Sodano. client Paul Smith Limited. photographer/stylist Sandro Sodano. text** "annual gift catalogue detailing the accessories available at Paul Smith stores, listing prices and availability. Distributed to UK/USA mailing lists." **page one hundred and forty nine**

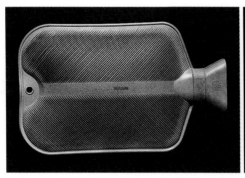

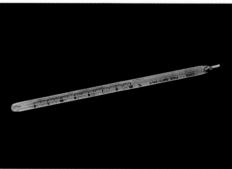

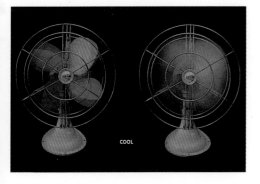

COOL

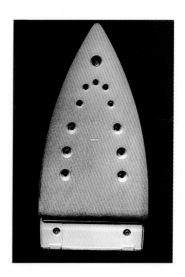

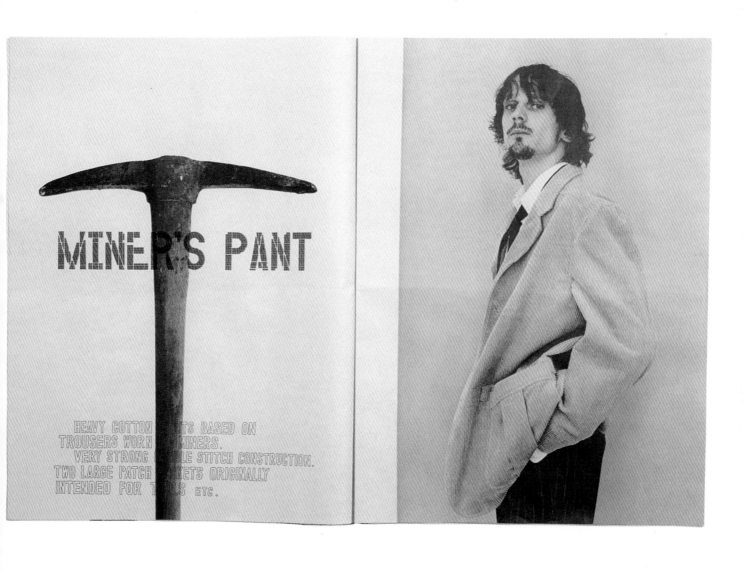

MINER'S PANT

HEAVY COTTON ☐TS BASED ON
TROUSERS WORN ☐MINERS.
VERY STRONG ☐LE STITCH CONSTRUCTION.
TWO LARGE PATCH ☐KETS ORIGINALLY
INTENDED FOR T☐LS ETC.

project catalogue,
advertising images. **title R Newbold spring/summer 1995. art director Alan K Aboud. design company Aboud Sodano. client Paul Smith Limited. photographer Julian Broad. typographer Tim Spencer. stylist Håkan Rosenius. hair Peter Smith.** project catalogue. **title R Newbold autumn/winter 1993. art director Alan K Aboud. design company Aboud Sodano. client Paul Smith Limited. photographer Sandro Sodano.** project newspaper catalogue, advertising images. **title R Newbold autumn/winter 1994. art director Alan K Aboud. design company Aboud Sodano. client Paul Smith Limited. photographer Julian Broad. typographers Tim Spencer, Nick Foley-Oates. stylist Håkan Rosenius. hair Peter Smith. qoute Alan K Aboud** "Newbolds...it's very different, it's much more what I want to do with typography and it's more abstract, but still featuring product. We've made a decision that every brochure is going to be a different format to make it collectable. Newbolds is for a younger market and they want to see something different every season otherwise they'll move on to the next big thing. It's selling incredibly well in Japan, they buy two of everything because it's so cheap, one to keep and one to wear." **page one hundred and fifty three**

URSULA CONZEN

URSULA CONZEN

REGARD (S)

project catalogue, loose front and back cover. **title regard(s) Ursula Conzen. designer Pippo Rondolotti. art director Franca Soncini. agency Soncini and Ginepro Europa. client Ursula Conzen. year 1993. photographer David Sims. stylist/casting Annett Monheim. hair Guido. make-up Miranda Joyce. text** "these images show a world of girls of our time. Looking at their faces it is hard to miss an underlying quality: the innocence shining through their eyes." **project catalogue, painted newsprint cover. title Rouge à Levres autumn/winter 1994. designer Pippo Rondolotti. art director Franca Soncini. agency Soncini and Ginepro Europa. client Rouge à Levres. photographer Alistair Taylor Young. stylist Susanne Gunther. hair Drew Jarrett at Atlantis. make-up Diane Kendal at Atlantic. page one hundred and fifty five**

Outside Window Rock (Arizona)

Elaine and Lynne, Wigley (Osage/Cherokee), Zia Pueblo

project catalogue. title native american indians Alberto Aspesi spring/summer 1994. designer Pippo Rondolotti. art director Franca Soncini. agency Soncini and Ginepro Europa. client Alberto Aspesi. photographer Ken Griffiths. project catalogue. title Alberto Aspesi. art director Franca Soncini. agency Soncini and Ginepro Europa. client Alberto Aspesi. photographer Robert Frank. page one hundred and fifty seven

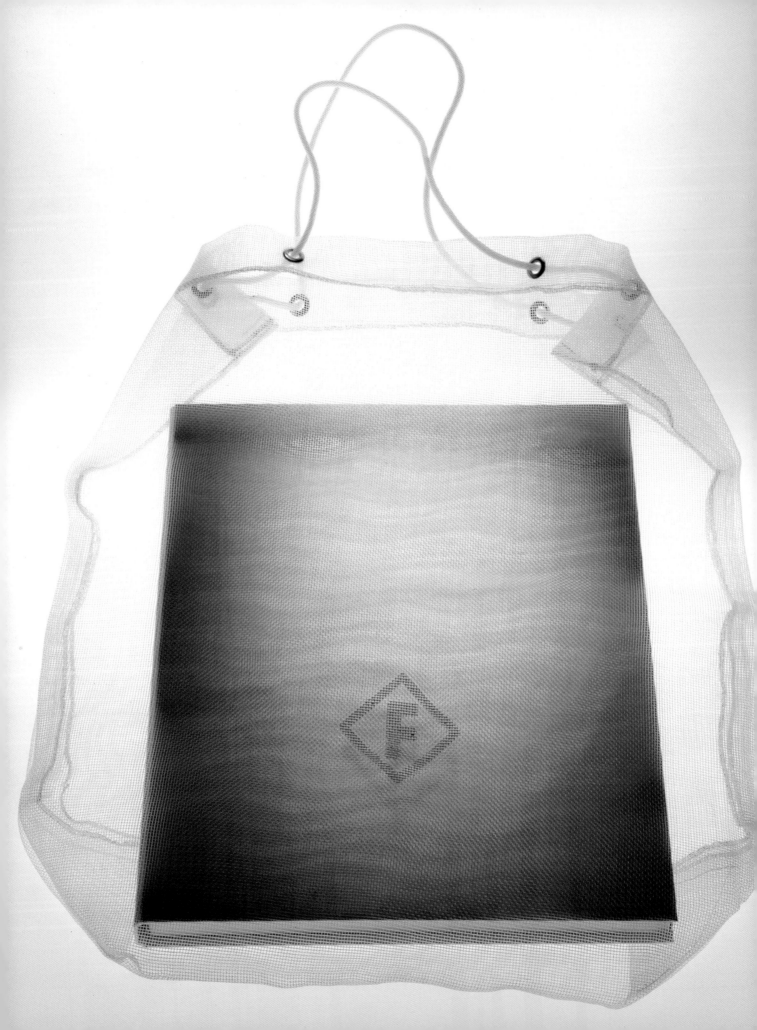

project catalogue in bag. **title Forum autumn/winter 1995.**
art directors/designers Giovanni Bianco, Susanna Cucco. design company Bianco & Cucco. client Forum Brazil. photographers André Andrade, Emmanuelle Bernard, Willy Biondani. copywriter João Carrascosa. project catalogue in bag. **title D&G spring/summer 1995. art directors/designers Giovanni Bianco, Susanna Cucco. design company Bianco & Cucco. client Ittierre for D&G Dolce & Gabbana. photographer Paolo Leone. computer-generated images Antonella Porfido. copy writer Francesca Pagliarini. page one hundred and fifty nine**

ART DIRECTION AND DE
BY FARRINGTON ASSOC
PHOTOGRAPHY BY NIN
SCHULTZ. STYLING BY C
KASTERINE. MAKE-UP B
KRYST. HAIR BY JIMO. M
CLARE MULHOLLAND, K
MARTIN, SARAH MURRA
OLOK. SHOT ON LOCAT
THE ISLE OF SHEPPEY A
WEST HOUSE. GLEBE P
LONDON. STILL-LIFE
PHOTOGRAPHY BY DAV
DOWNIE. CATALOGUE P
BY FIRST IMPRESSION.
LONDON. ON CHLORINE
ENVIRONMENTALLY FRI
PAPER.

1966–83

In 1966 it was rare for an apparel manufacturer to launch an advertising campaign, but Benetton invested in corporate advertising even then. Until 1983, Benetton's advertising was limited to two countries, Italy and France. The nature of this advertising was clearly product-oriented, showing the product and nothing else. In 1984, Benetton's advertising reached America with New York Magazine carrying the "Benetton's Colorful Summer Cotton" ad.

Benetton ha iniziato a investire nella pubblicità fin dal 1966, quando ancora la pubblicità da parte delle aziende del settore dell'abbigliamento era assai rara. Fino al 1983, la pubblicità di Benetton veniva diffusa solamente in due Paesi, l'Italia e la Francia, e l'immagine presentata si limitava a "far vedere" i prodotti. Nel 1984 l'azienda entra nel mercato americano, e presenta sulla rivista New York Magazine una pubblicità dal titolo "Cotone estivo multicolore di Benetton".

1984

In the spring of 1984, a new communication strategy transformed Benetton advertising. Photographer Oliviero Toscani was brought in and with Parisian advertising agency Eldorado he started to give Benetton's advertising a new face. The first "hit" was "All the Colors of the World". It provided food for thought with its images of happy faces, the faces of racially different children, all laughing and smiling together. The ad campaign was run in 14 countries and its slogan was translated into all the various languages. Its message struck home: "Stratégie", a French advertising magazine, awarded it the Grand Prix de la Publicité.

Nella primavera del 1984, sulla base di una nuova strategia di comunicazione, ha inizio una campagna pubblicitaria che si avvale dell'opera del fotografo Oliviero Toscani, prodotta dall'agenzia di pubblicità Eldorado di Parigi. La prima fase di questa pubblicità si intitola "Tutti i colori del mondo": una serie dedicata a visi di bambini di varie razze che ridono tutti insieme. La pubblicità viene diffusa in 14 paesi, con lo slogan tradotto nella lingua di ciascun paese. La pubblicità venne aggiudicato il Gran Premio pubblicitario della rivista francese "Stratégie", specializzata in pubblicità industriale.

1985

This is the year the slogan "United Colors of Benetton" is born. This slogan will not only be repeated in successive years but it will also eventually become the new trade-mark of the company.
The campaign develops: colors and nationalities are mixed, flags and symbols of various countries are added, the people are all happy and smiling. The images seem to be a call for peace in the world.

È l'anno in cui nasce lo slogan "United Colors of Benetton", che viene non solo mantenuto anche negli anni futuri, ma finisce per diventare il marchio di fabbrica di Benetton. Il tema è la fusione di colori e nazionalità diverse. In ogni fotografia vengono raffigurate persone di vari paesi, sorridenti e felici, insieme con le bandiere e con i simboli dei singoli paesi. Un'immagine che richiama la pace nel mondo.

1986

The main theme of the new Benetton campaign is the globe. By choosing models with accentuated ethnic features and names written in their own languages, the campaign strives for and achieves an image which is even more multiracial and international. Although they are dressed in Benetton products, the models seem to be wearing national costumes.

Viene realizzata una nuova campagna con la terra come simbolo, un'immagine multirazziale e internazionale. A questo scopo i modelli sono ritratti con un carattere etnico che sembra accentuare le singole caratteristiche, ed il proprio nome scritto nella lingua originale del paese. L'abito indossato dai modelli è di produzione Benetton, ma sembra un costume di carattere popolare, tradizionale e folcloristico.

1987

The Fall/Winter campaign carries the slogan "United Fashions of Benetton". The pictures portray young people dressed in Benetton clothes but with accessories that reflect the style of the great names in fashion.

Lo slogan per la campagna autunno/inverno 1987 è "United Fashions of Benetton". Si tratta di ritratti di giovani vestiti con prodotti Benetton, ciascuno dei quali indossa accessori che fanno chiaramente comprendere lo stile dei grandi nomi del mondo della moda.

1988

"United Superstars" is the slogan for the Spring/Summer campaign. Joan of Arc and Marilyn Monroe, Leonardo da Vinci and Julius Caesar, Adam and Eve, are portrayed alongside each other. Once again, a mixture of history and culture.

Lo slogan per la campagna primavera/estate 1988 è "United Superstars". Sono fotografati insieme, Giovanna d'Arco, Marilyn Monroe, Leonardo da Vinci, Giulio Cesare, Adamo ed Eva. Un nuovo suggestivo insieme di storia e cultura.

ADVERTISING

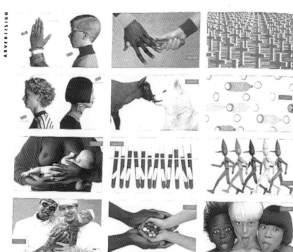

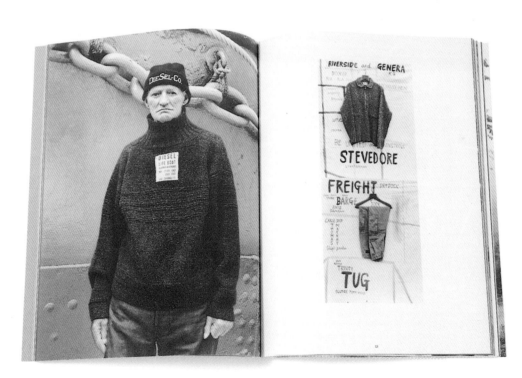

Diesel autumn/winter 1993. designers Brian Baderman, Nick Foley-Oates. design company Baderman. client Diesel. photographers Matthew R Lewis, Mike Smith, Donald Milne, Nigel Shafran, Craig Richards, Nigel Henry Case. illustrator Craig Richards. page one hundred and sixty five

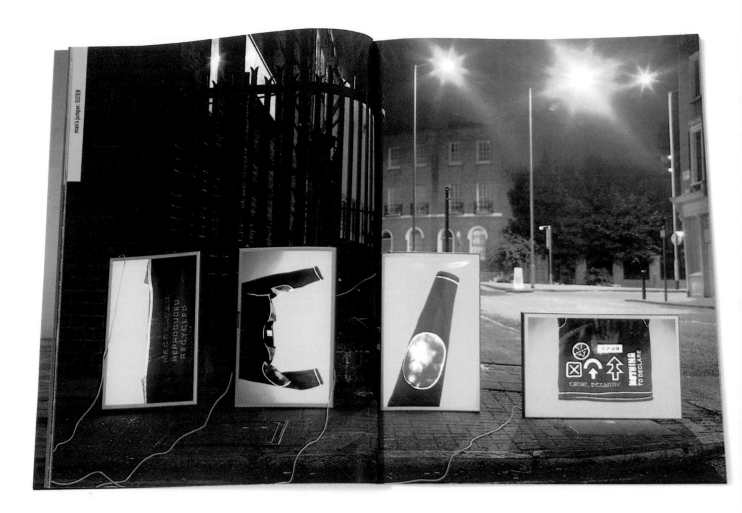

project catalogue. **title Diesel spring/summer 1994. designers Brian Baderman, Nick Foley-Oates, Dan Adams. design company Baderman. client Diesel. photography Sandro Sodano, Nigel Case, Jake Chessum, Michael Croft, Nathan Ward, Donald Christie, Glyn Howells, Gautier Deblonde, Nicholas Foley-Oates, Brian Baderman. stylist Liz Botes. hair Lyn Barry.** project (and over leaf) catalogue. **title Diesel autumn/winter 1994. designers Brian Baderman, Adam Whitaker, Adrian Philpott, Tim Hutchinson. design company Baderman. client Diesel. photographers Sandro Sodano, Pierre Winther, Brian Baderman. stylist Liz Botes. quote Brian Baderman** "when I went to see the clothing designers to discuss doing a catalogue they were so exhausted from having done the collection they just chose the best pieces of clothing and told me to get on with it, quickly. After the first couple of years there was a rapport and confidence which has lasted until today. To begin with it was very much a product-based company, they were very good at selling and manufacturing, but they **were very** good above all at researching their product, they had huge ranges at the beginning of each season, it was never ten or twenty or **thirty** items, it was always hundreds of items. And it was always very interesting finding lots of details on the products, like finishes and linings of different materials and lots of extra pockets and buttons and different forms of closures, so to some extent when I look back on the early catalogues the same mentality seems **to be present in the graphics,** almost an obsessive attention to detail, over-loaded with information.

For at least four or five years there was a lot **of collage** work and they only saw **collaged** up photocopies before the photographs were taken because at that point the clothes were only **shown as** still-lifes, no models. We **photocopied** the actual clothes, but then there were more and more things done to the clothes, put **in unusual** positions, unusual situations. So for two or three years the client has only seen the catalogue at proofing stage when it's too late to change anything, which is a compliment but also a responsibility. It shouldn't be over-sophisticated and I like the idea of having lots of jokes that people have to work at a little bit to read, and that means they get more involved and you kind of create a whole world around this product.

I felt that if you were creating an image around this you could create something that was very thorough, so to some extend that's me, I brought what I knew to it. There's no market research even now, incredible a company that size doesn't do any market research. But over the last couple of years, as the marketing director himself says, they've shifted from being a product-based company to being an image-based company because that seems to be the only way companies can grow past a certain point. They have got to be able to give it presence in people's minds on a larger scale and that can only be done by abstracting it into images whether it's in a catalogue or adverts." **page one hundred and sixty seven**

COMMON WATER CARRIER, CONDITIONS; PER LITER

trousers: ENTRY top: CHARY shoes: YUK

le Panic

T SERVICE ROOM #11 [LUXURY]
NE CLEAN GENT'S JACKET
PRICE [INC. DEL.] $30

le Panic

VALET SERVICE ROOM #17 [AVERAGE]
ONE CLEAN GENT'S JACKET
PRICE [INC. DEL.] A PUNCH IN THE FACE

t: Burns

Jacket: Challis

project catalogue. title Diesel spring/summer
1995. designers Brian Baderman, Adam Whitaker, Miles English. design company Baderman (pages 1-11 and 85-95 by Paradiset Sweden).
client Diesel. photographers Henrik Halvarsson, Ellen Von Unwerth. typographer Adam Whitaker. stylist Liz Botes. quote Brian Baderman "as
every catalogue changes, and circumstances with the client change, there was more of an attempt to write a unified whole thing from
beginning to end, because one of the strengths, and weaknesses, of earlier catalogues have been the number of disparate images page
after page that don't follow any kind of continuum that maybe surprise but maybe don't and are very fractured. But this time there was a
scenario and there were characters the models had to play. They felt that the perception of Diesel as a manufacturer of women's clothing
needed to be heightened. That dictated the use of a lot more models, because womens' clothing, especially if it's kind of figure-hugging
summer clothing, needs to be shown on good-looking people to make the clothes look good. Time was very short and they agreed with me,
that it wasn't a good idea to try to do another summer catalogue in London during the winter. We had to do all the photography in ten days in
Miami. Why Miami? Because of the sun, and there was this derelict hotel we used quite a lot of the time." **page one hundred and seventy one**

project catalogue. **title towards the sea Fire and Ice spring / summer 1994. art director Terry Jones. designers Omaid Hiwaizi, Matt Brooke. design company Instant Design Studio. client Willy Bogner, Fire and Ice. agency .start advertising. photographers Stefan Ruiz, Thomas Kalak. video and film maker Dominique Lutier. producers Uli Wiesmeier, Tricia Jones. words Kayt Jones. quote Terry Jones** "the clients didn't know how it would work and actually it's only just really sinking in that it is working, because it's basically using their whole advertising budget and putting everything in to a limited edition of 8,000 books. We've done a very small ad campaign that comes out of the shoot. There are two trips a year, one each season, after they've finished their selling period, – because it's not a catalogue to try and sell to trade – it's completely promotional. There's nothing else like it, the idea of taking a group of mixed international people on a trip. We give them the worst scenario. For the winter catalogue one of the forms of transport is snowboards so they have to be competent snowboarders, they have to be able to do double diamonds off piste without endangering any lives.

This was a travel journey, more like the book of the movie. There were things that happened on the trip and we just documented it. There's no stylist, they have to wear the clothes that are in the bag and by the end of the day they're swapping clothes around. I had some rain jackets so I said, 'OK, lets go for a swim', and the client got really pissed off, because they're expensive clothes, it was partly because of the state that they came back in, he couldn't sell them. I think art direction is a collaboration, I'd always have an idea of who I felt was right for the package on a shoot. It's the conceptual idea that has to be carried through, so for Fire and Ice I use a photographer who is essentially a portrait photographer. Because I was shooting the video that led the direction of the photography. It is a situation thing, and often you'd stop at a place and something would happen and usually the video would pick up the thing before a still, a still would have to pull those things into a one picture idea and sometimes that's really difficult." project postcard. **title apply now! Fire and Ice. art director Terry Jones. design company Instant Design Studio. client Willy Bogner, Fire and Ice. text on reverse** "be part of our next real life adventure. Send a picture and your personal details to: Fire and Ice, St. Veit - Str. 4, 81673 München, Germany". **page one hundred and seventy three**

FEEL THE FORCE OF NATURE

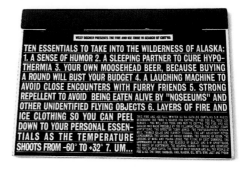

project catalogue. title where the hell is chit'na? Fire and Ice fall/winter 1993. art director Terry Jones. art assistant Petra Langhammer. design company Instant Design Studio. client Willy Bogner, Fire and Ice. agency .start advertising. photographers Stefan Ruiz, Thomas Kalak, Vianney Tisseau. page one hundred and seventy five

FASHION MAGAZINE N°I 50p

i-D

project magazine. title *i-D* no 1 1980. editors

Perry Haines, Terry Jones, Al McDowell. photographers Steve Johnson, Peter Ashworth, Paul Brammer, Simon Brown, Brian Griffin, Paul McKay, James Palmer, Patrick Sarfati. publisher T J Informat Design Limited. text on back cover "*i-D* is a Fashion/Style Magazine. Style isn't what but how you wear clothes. Fashion is the way you walk, talk, dance and prance. Through *i-D* ideas travel fast and free of the mainstream – so join us on the run!" **quote Terry Jones** "*i-D* is about people who are fans of fashion, stopping them and photographing them on the street. I went to the guy who was doing fanzines, a guy called Jolly in a company called Better Badges, and he was the main fanzine printer and I said I want to do a fanzine about fashion and he was a really cool guy, a real hippie and he said 'OK, what the deal is, if I print them you buy copies off me and we'll do 2,000 to begin with'. His outlets were record shops. He had his distribution through Rough Trade and I ended up buying a 1,000 or more of the first one and he got rid of the others and I started building up distribution. Newsagents complained about the staples, people were piercing their fingers and getting blood on the other magazines, and I ended up with two newsagents which still took the second and third issues and then we got Virgin to start taking it, and it just grew from there, but they were still delivered to the house. I'd go out and do the fly-posting. Initially it was fine, it was a hobby...everyone who got involved in it put a huge amount of energy into it, it was a total collaboration, it was always done late at night and it got to the point where the house was full of people all the time. Most of my work was abroad, I was out of the country up to three weeks out of a month. When I came back then we'd do the magazine. Initially I just had a golfball typewriter so we had a range of four golfballs and then bit by bit the characters would start dropping off. We used to get the photocopies done up the road and most of the design was through physical necessity because we just worked with the things that we had. Steve Johnson was the photographer and we had a darkroom downstairs. Another guy called James Palmer had a VW and used to drive around the UK and take pictures. We did the first issue with club pictures and also stopping people in the street and I needed one shot, so we had two shots per person. The first set of contacts we had were absolutely brilliant because they were just treating the camera like a documentary tool but it became a little bit formalised, people looked like a police file. It was still a classic format but I wanted them to start getting a bit more energy into it. Then Fiorucci asked me to be their art director and that way I was able to pay people a salary, so when people like Caryn Franklin left college and Moira Bogue and Steve Male, who was an illustrator, the first job they worked on was a series of stickers I did for Fiorucci. I had this idea of doing electronic romance so I bought a computer, an Apple 2E and I needed someone to operate it and that's how I found Robin Derrick. He was just starting to do stuff on computer at college and he put me in touch with people who had a bitmap, because I needed to have a pen you could draw with. Moira was still at college and I met her because she came to do her thesis on *i-D*. I always saw my role in *i-D* like the catalyst because what was important was to steer the creative energy of a lot of different people to produce something they were satisfied with and thought was worthwhile to work on, so at the end the magazine was the creation of whoever was involved in it at that time, it was never a single person, it was just that I knew what I wanted to have conceptually as a magazine. It was a very simple formula, stopping people in the street and instead of having journalists saying 'this is what you've got to do' it was that the people we photographed were saying 'this is what I'm interested in'. If we photographed someone and put them in the magazine it was because they looked interesting and had something interesting to say and they weren't in there just as a kind of decorative object. They were there because we wanted to find out a little bit about them so that's why we always had this questionnaire, name, profession, likes, dislikes, music. From the early issues I had stylists like Caroline Baker doing a fashion prediction and the involvement of other people who would put looks together. The idea was to promote new talent, so for instance Caryn was a graphic designer but in the end I said she was the right person to pick people because she always looked so good herself, she had a good eye, she should go out with a photographer and find who she thought was interesting and then if we needed to photograph some clothes she was always the one who did the styling, she shifted out of being a designer to doing that. I'm not a decorator, I never got in to the decorative kind of graphics thing, but for instance, when the magazine went through a stage where we did things faster...the aesthetic relationship of things that was Moira's bag and Tim Hopgood brought this kind of hand feel, basically he was a painter and brought a painterly quality into the design and the same with Steve. He had no interest in type at all, but I always like to take people who don't have a traditional approach to how you had to treat type. My background was more traditional in that I had in mind the Bauhaus idea of always minimalise everything, more than three typefaces is what you don't do, so immediately I'd use five, I'd do the bad taste thing as a reaction to what people were teaching me, and when I had someone like a painter or an illustrator involved in type I'd bring their aesthetic skills of balance into the design, so the whole design was looser. The first guy who worked on the magazine, Ally McDowell, was a painter that I met, he was a student, a punk painter, when I was doing the punk book and he had his show torn down because of the content. It was actually closed down by the police. He became a really good friend and he was doing the t-shirts for Vivienne Westwood, like the two cowboys one, so he had a print background. And because of his connection inside the music field there were people, like Steve Strange, who were in the first issue, that's how *i-D* kind of begun really." **page one hundred and seventy seven**

spread. title scorched *i-D* no 37 June 1986. art director Terry Jones. art editor Moira Bogue. designer Tim Hopgood. photographer Nick Knight. stylist Simon Foxton. project 21-page fashion story. title superbad! *i-D* no 49 July 1987. art director Terry Jones. art editor/designer Stephen Male. designers Paul Eustace, Corinna Farrow. photographer Nick Knight. styling Simon Foxton. hair Kevin Ryan at Antenna, Martyn F Calder at Faces. make-up David Grainger. project eight-page fashion story. title say it loud! *i-D* no 70 June 1989. editor-in-chief Terry Jones. art director Stephen Male. art editor Neil Edwards. designers Paul Baptiste, Mike Foley, Damon Murray, Raj-Seo-Chavda. photographer Kate Garner at Satellite. stylist Claire Hall at Satellite. hair Jonathan Connelly at Opera. make-up Pat Magrath at Unique. project eight-page story. title viva! *i-D* no 98 November 1991. editor-in-chief Terry Jones. art director Stephen Male. art editor Corinne Farrow. design editor Omaid Hiwaizi. design assistants Paul Baptiste, Paul Khera. photographer Xavier Guardans. project 18-page fashion story. title the outsiders *i-D* no 78 March 1990. editor-in-chief Terry Jones. art director/designer Stephen Male. art editor/designer Neil Edwards. designer Paul Baptiste. photographer Ronald Stoops. words Kayt Jones. project six-page fashion story. title blue movie a fashion thriller by Jean Colonna. *i-D* no 127 April 1994. editor-in-chief Terry Jones. art director Scott King. art editor Corinna Farrow. art assistant Matt Brooke. art director/concept/stylist Jean Colonna. photographer Juergen Teller. quote Terry Jones "I was kind of training designers up. At the point where it becomes a collaboration, and I feel someone is right to let loose on the design, it's to do with relationship of scale, because I like contrast. Each person that has worked on the magazine has used devices that are part of what I call the tool box of graphics, but they use them in their way. They bring their hand skill into it." quote Judy Blame "I don't know whether *i-D* created careers and I don't know if it's got anything to do with business but it's got to do with awareness. I mean when I first started styling and I said it was for *i-D* you wouldn't believe how many doors slammed in my face. Well now if I call up and say it's *i-D* I can get Versace's door open, I can get Armani's, I can get anyone in the world's door open now because they're all desperate to be in *i-D*, they don't want to be considered old-fashioned. But when I first started, apart from the English designers, they would say, 'oh we're not doing *i-D*, funny printing, dodgy paper, bad photographers', it was really snobbish...and with girls like Kate Moss and everyone who all started with us, they're all icons of an era now, it's swings and roundabouts." **page one hundred and seventy nine**

Nine million tonnes of ... you can tell where because of the dead fish and hospital waste floating on the surf...

FELIX wears jacket by Christopher Nemeth

project 14-page fashion story. title dying waters *i-D* **no 80 May 1990. editor-in-chief Terry Jones. art director/designer Stephen Male. art editor/designer Neil Edwards. designer Paul Baptiste. photographer Jean Baptiste Mondino. still-life Craig McDean. stylist Judy Blame. hair Mark Lopez at Brigitte Hébant. make-up Christophe at Brigitte Hébant. casting Gigi Lepage, Jeremy. text** "nine million tonnes of sewage is dumped off New York's coast – you can tell where because of the dead fish and hospital waste floating on the surface. In a government experiment, one in ten people who swam off a Welsh beach reported stomach upsets or nausea three days after." **project 12-page fashion story. title visions** *i-D* **no 92 May 1991. editor-in-cheif Terry Jones. art director/designer Stephen Male. designers Omaid Hiwaizi, Paul Baptiste, Paul Khera, Rebecca Velten, Nathan Brandon. photographer Juergen Teller. stylist Judy Blame. fashion assistant Emma Day. hair Marc Lopez at Brigitte Hébant. quote Judy Blame** "the pollution story, that was when I really knew I was cracking it. That's when I took a fashion story out of context and tried to make people think about it, but also make attractive and dangerous images, you have to look at it, you're drawn in by it and then you actually read the facts. It's all about what's happening to the water and what we're taking out of the water, and eating out of the water, so that's why I put in all the knives and forks and razor blades and flowers, and a bit of a dig at America. I wanted the models to look like birds pulled out of the sea because the Exon disaster had happened a couple of months before and I kept seeing news footage. I made this bra up of broken records and bits of string. That was a Friends of the Earth t-shirt I bought at Camden Market and I wanted to get some sort of corporate image, the big corporations do shag up the world.

I walk a thin line between two worlds, but I want to say something. I thought I could do a shoot about the homeless, but that was too thin a line for even me to walk on, do the same thing like pollution but with a homeless theme, and we did six days shooting on that and it still wasn't right. I couldn't live with myself, I was using expensive clothes. I love the shoot and it was one of Juergen Teller's best, and it was very much about the people in the end. The way the pollution story was right in your face and very obvious I couldn't do it with that, it was an insult, so we turned it more towards art and portraits, spent a lot of time doing the layouts. One of my favourite photographs was a £500 Galliano suit and I just wopped the *Financial Times* right under it and wrapped the *Daily Mirror* round her head with a bit of string, and that's what we're going to have to look like if we don't solve a few of those problems." **page one hundred and eighty one**

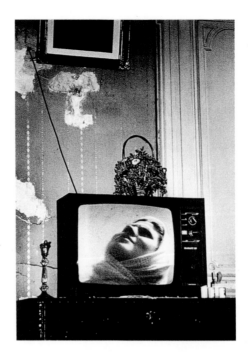

Juergen Teller · Photographs
ヨーガン・テラー 写真展

 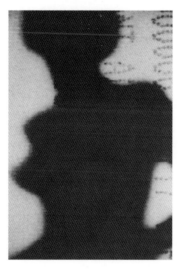  

project photography exhibition catalogue. **title Juergen Teller Photographs. designer/typographer Cornel Windlin. client Exposure Parco Photographers Gallery Tokyo. year 1992. photographer Juergen Teller. text** "Romania 1990. Fashion story by Venetia Scott. Published in *i-D* magazine. Card no 9 of a set of 31. Yohji Yamamoto backstage, Paris 1991. For *03 Tokyo Calling* magazine. Card no 23 of a set of 31." project *Visionaire* no 7 black fall 1992. **title Cecilia photographed by Gan. photographer Stephen Gan. hair/make-up James Kaliardos at Visages. model Cecilia Dean at Click. title cat. photographer Stephen Gan. title dog. illustrator Mats Gustafson at Art & Commerce. title woman. photographer Philippe Salomon. comment** "two projects consisting of fashion-inspired images art directed/collated into a format which enables the viewer to re-sequence the contents and make their own connections between images." **page one hundred and eighty three**

project lay-out for fashion story. title George *Ray Gun* October 1994. art directors Phil Bicker, Corinne Day. photographer Corinne Day.
comment "Corinne Day lived with and photographed the subject, George, over a number of days. Phil and Corinne scanned in the photographs and ordered them on screen before supplying them on disc to David Carson the art director of *Ray Gun*." **page one hundred and eighty five**

Steven Meisel
New York City, May 1994
For Calvin Klein

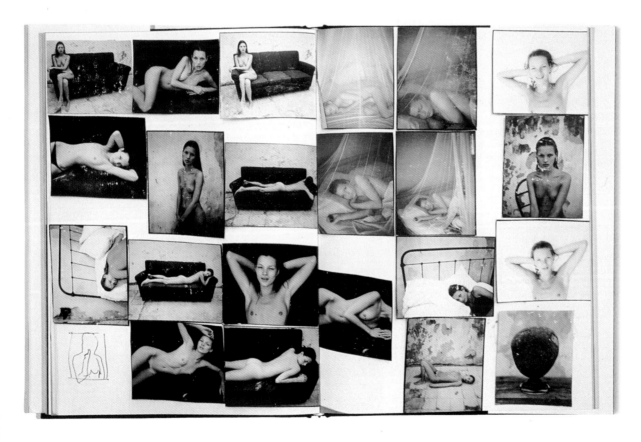

kate

title *kate*. designer Phil Bicker. production Jessica Hallett. author Kate Moss. foreword Liz Tilberis. publisher Pavilion Books Limited. year 1995. photographers Steven Meisel and Mario Sorrenti for Calvin Klein. cover photographer Corinne Day. page one hundred and eighty seven

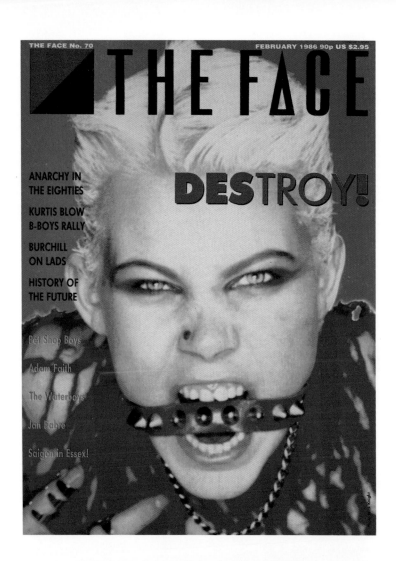

project cover, fashion story. **title ten years of punk** *The Face* **February 1986. art director/ typographer Robin Derrick. photographer Nick Knight. stylist Simon Foxton. comment** "anticipating a trend *The Face* celebrated the tenth anniversary of punk rock. Robin Derrick commissioned photographer Nick Knight to add a veneer of 1980s gloss, wedding saturated colour and hard-edged technology to the punk attitude. Punk had entered the vocabulary of fashion, it was no long simply a past genre of pop. A few years later a new generation of fashion designers would adopt this hybrid mix of high and low tech to produce a futuristic revival."

project cover, fashion story. **title glamour is back**

Vogue **November 1993. art director Robin Derrick. photographer Nick Knight. stylist Lucinda Chambers. comment** "a fashion story that was originally planned as 'new Victorians' was transformed by the combination of art direction and photography. Robin Derrick and Nick Knight referred to 1970s fashion photography and in particular a story which Helmut Newton shot for *Nova* April 1973, with a flying drink caught in a ring-flash before a gloss-painted backdrop, evoking a mood of claustrophobic sleaze. By adding the cover line 'glamour is back' Robin Derrick anticipated the end of grunge and the re-emergence of glamour a few seasons before the catwalk shows proved him right." **project magazine cover. title** *Blow.* **designers 10x5. year 1994-1995. comment** "10x5 re-use a high-point from the history of fashion magazines updating another *Nova* first for the 1990s. The format, of a melancholy woman whose thoughts are the cover lines comes from *Nova* September 1968. The 1960s version read, 'I have taken the pill. I have hoisted my skirts to my thighs, dropped them to my ankles, rebelled at university, abused the American Embassy, lived with two men, married one, earned my keep, kept my identity and frankly…I'm lost'." **page one hundred and eighty nine**

This instructive video-cassette can help overcome daily household boredom.
The hot-pink Lycra catsuit by Veronique Leroy can conveniently be obtained using your
personal code. Order now and receive one of three elegant bonus gifts:
* Acrylic chainbelt with matching boots by Veronique Leroy
* Designer earrings by YSL
* High-tech ladies wrist watch by Pulsar

project 11-page fashion story. **title global warming tv** *The Face* **no 72 September 1994. art director Lee Swillingham. designers/typographers Lee Swillingham, Stuart Spalding. photographer Inez Van Lamsweerde. image manipulation Kim Mannes-Abbott. graphic Paintbox facilities Colourspace. backgrounds Zefa. stylist Vinoodh Matadin. hair/make-up Ellis Faas at Corinne's Agency. text** "Inez Van Lamsweerde and Vinoodh Matadin are a team creating images 'about fashion and the way it influences our lives, gives us certain ideals and stereotypes'. The models here were photographed in the studio, then superimposed on background library shots using the Paintbox computer system...On global warming tv, nothing is as it seems". **comment** "Lee Swillingham at *The Face* is championing a new generation of technically-innovative photographers. He works alongside them story-boarding each shoot before the photographer creates or sources the separate elements. Then the pair retreat to a facilities house to digitally combine, doctor and enhance the final images." **page one hundred and ninety one**

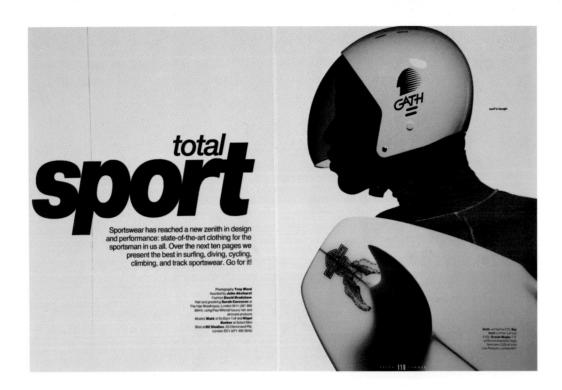

total
sport

Sportswear has reached a new zenith in design and performance: state-of-the-art clothing for the sportsman in us all. Over the next ten pages we present the best in surfing, diving, cycling, climbing, and track sportswear. Go for it!

Photography **Troy Word**
Assisted by **John Akehurst**
Fashion **David Bradshaw**
Hair and grooming **Sarah Corcoran** at
The Hair Warehouse, London W11 (281 950
8849), using Paul Mitchell luxury hair and
skincare products
Models **Waló** at So Darn Tuff and **Nigel
Barker** at Select Men
Shot at **B2 Studios**, 63 Clerkenwell Rd,
London EC1 (071 490 2845)

surf's tough

Gath surf helmet £19, **Rip
Curl** summer surf suit
£129. **Ocean Magic** 7'2"
surfboard shaped by Nigel
Sommers £325 all from
Low Pressure, London W11

This page and opposite
Lithuanian Olympic Uniforms
specially designed by **Issey
Miyako** for the Olympic
Games (see Vianety), skin
freshened with Paul Mitchell
Awapuhi Moisture Mist

speed freak

This page: Zoom Sprint shoes
£49.99 by **Nike** from Olympus
Sport nationwide

Opposite page: **Ocean
Magic** surfboard (over £72).
Rip Curl summer surf suit
£129, cloth from Low Pressure,
London W11, skin scrub blast
with Paul Mitchell Foaming
Pomade

**For stockists' details see
Directory**

project fashion story. **title total sport *Arena* summer 1992. art director/typographer Robin Derrick. photographer Troy Word. stylist David Bradshaw.** project nine-page fashion story. **title winning *Dazed & Confused* no 8 1994. designer Ian C Taylor. design company The Artificial Sweetener. photographer Rankin. stylist Katie Grand. comment** "fashion magazines have been instrumental in introducing sportswear to new audiences. Aimed at two very different readerships, the approach of the art director differentiates clothes primarily designed for the same purpose, performance." **page one hundred and ninety three**

fancy a shag *Another* no 1 1994. art director/designer Gerard Saint. design company Big-Active Limited. typography Gerard Saint, Donald Milne.

photography by donald milne, styling by bob hazarde at owl workshop, hair by johnny sappong, make up by hina dohi. the people in the photographs are jj (so dam tuff) tabitha (select) and maria (select) thanks to krista (bookings), simon, rachel and ben. 'bitch lust' t-shirt by merry pranksters 'rollerball' t-shirt by prof. head available at the duffer shop. all other clothes were bought in thrift shops in san fransisco
↓ simon

©donald milne 1994

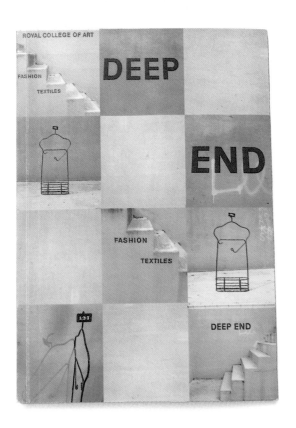

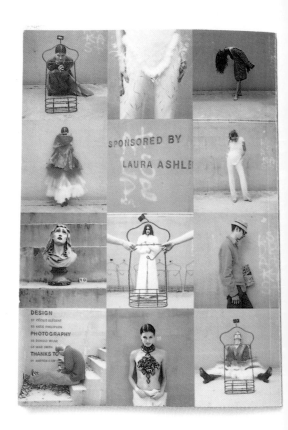

PRINTED TEXTILES

project fashion graduates' catalogue. title deep end, Royal College of Art fashion catalogue 1993. designers Katie Phillipson, Cécile Blégent. client School of Fashion and Textiles. photographers Donald Milne, Mike Smith. sign writing Andrew Gibb. page one hundred and ninety nine

Fashioncatalogue1994

124 Willow Vale
London W12 OPB
t: 0181 248 2030

Thanks to Phoebe

Collection:
'Sculpted Synthetics'

4

Isabel Dodd
Embroidery

project fashion graduates' catalogue. **title Royal College of Art fashion catalogue 1994. art directors/typographers Violetta Suzzet Boxill, David Revell. client School of Fashion and Textiles. photographer Matthew Andrews. stylist Francesca Bartolli. hair Vidal Sassoon. make-up Shu Uemara.** project fashion graduates' catalogue. **title Royal College of Art fashion catalogue 1995. art directors Leila Naaman, Patricia Hepp. client School of Fashion and Textiles. photography/digital imaging Phillips & Laurent. hair Peter Gray at Vidal Sassoon. make-up Bobbi Brown at Professional Cosmetics. page two hundred and one**

VOGUE
DEUTSCH

Condé Nast Verlag Gmbh
Ainmillerstr. 8
80801 München

Phone: 011-49-89/38 10 40 Fax: 011-49-89/38 10 42 30 Telex: 52 81 88 grog d

Date __4/27/94__

Address __BIG-Magazine__

Attention to __Marcelo Jünemann__

Telefax __(212) 645-9467__

From __Donald Schneider__

Pages __17__

Hi Marcelo, here it is!
Best — D-ld

27 APR '94 21:40 CONDE NAST VERLAG

CONDE NAST VERLAG S.2
27 APR '94 21:39

project eight-page feature. title Donald Schneider *Big* no 10 direction issue. art director/typographer Vince Frost. design company Frost Design. client *Big* magazine. year 1995. page two hundred and three

TALISMAN MAKERS. FASHION DERIVED
FROM THE LANGUAGE OF GRAPHICS.
GRAPHIC DESIGNERS TAKE TO THE
CLOTH. THE CANVAS OF THE 21ST
CENTURY IS THE T-SHIRT

bir th**of**th e**cool**

BIRTH OF THE COOL

project shop facade and interior. **title birth of the cool. designer/typographer Simon Taylor. design company Tomato.** **client urban re-action. year 1994. quote Simon Taylor** "the shop, I did it on the Mac before I went to Japan. When I got there I photocopied it all up. I wanted to make it all blue and really old because the outside of the shop and the whole street is quite run down, it's just varnished over, four metres long, two metres wide." project editorial photos. **designer Simon Taylor. design company Tomato. photographer Peter Ashworth.** project logo. **title URA. designer/typographer Simon Taylor. design company Tomato. client urban re-action. year 1995. quote Simon Taylor** "urban re-action might go to America and it is already happening in New Zealand and Australia so I don't particularly want my name pushed out in those markets, it's not fair on the people I'm working with, it's always been a collective thing. Urban reaction comes from the architect, David Green, he did a thing called tune up urban action, it's a little bit of an ode to him." **page two hundred and seven**

SPEEDNIK

EXILE

MODERN citizen

GOLDEN FIST

DOPE RHYME SLAYER

NEXUS
LOAFER

FLOAT LIKE A BUTTERFLY

STING LIKE A BEE

BEAUTIFULL POETRY
CHEAP SENTIMENT
all eyes open

project print designs. **title urban cowboys. designer/typographer Simon Taylor. design company Tomato. client urban re-action. year 1994. quote Simon Taylor** "I fax designs through and they print from them which is good fun. I've just done these new ones called urban cowboys, piccies of me, John, Dirk and Graham, drawn all over. In Japan, in this market, they like the idea that the stuff is from the UK or US. The general market isn't keen on reading their own language on t-shirts. Sam Peckinpah, urban cowboys, his life was like that, people who are maybe a little mis-directed by the moment but also have a role to play, that's kind of how I see urban cowboys. One season's designs are based on the same graphic with lots of variation. It's a continual turnover, new stuff every month. They can shift 1,000 t-shirts a month on a collection, the shops ask for new stuff, hassle them. For the first time ever they asked me to do urban cowboys, that was their idea. For the first three years they never asked me to do anything at all, I always said to them 'what's been the best seller and why?' and they say 'everything's a best seller because we print 5,000 and we sell them all', and if it's a really good one they'll just sell it then stop printing it." **project logo. title tubular technology. designer/typographer Simon Taylor. design company Tomato. client Adidas. year 1993. page two hundred and nine**

Before you go
do me a favour
give me that number
of that girl almost
      like you
with legs almost
      like you
I'm very deep into
    mass production
you're ~~not~~ nothing
       really
new.......

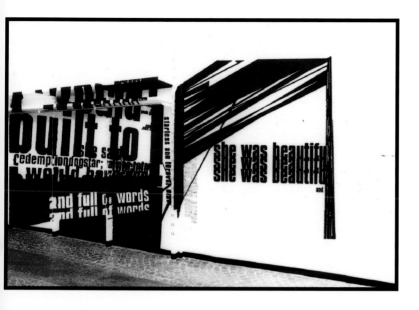

project installation, coat hanger, dress by Martin Margiela. title mass production. artist Maurizio Vetrugno. year 1994. text Iggy Pop. courtesy of Galleria SALES Rome. project shop interior. designers Maurizio Vetrugno, Tomato. client Jana. year 1994. page two hundred and eleven

project strapless dress, bodice made from pages of *The Complete Works of Shakespeare* and Made in England ribbon edged with souvenir key rings, skirt of laminated paper prints of the Royal Family bordered by the 'garden of England', 'train of thought' embroidered with thoughts on sartorial behaviour and codes. **title court couture. designers The New RenaisCAnce. photographer Zanna. text** "outfit designed for 'Court Couture' collection at Kensington Palace according to 1938 rules governing court dress. intended as a sartorial embodiment of British culture as perceived by visitors to this country." **project dress designed for Naomi Campbell, bodice of Sellotape and dollar bills, skirt of pages of the** *Financial Times*. **title Naomi Campbell's** *Financial Times*. **designers/stylists The New RenaisCAnce. year 1994. photographer Robert Fairer. project promotional image. title portrait of The New RenaisCAnce. designers/stylists The New RenaisCAnce. client British European Design Group,** *Blueprint*. **year 1993. photographers Mann & Man. hair/make-up Julie Thomas at Terri Mandura. comment** "image commissioned for the *In the swim* catalogue to accompany an exhibition of young British designers staged in Bremerhaven, Germany. The t-shirt is made of 'sequins' cut from a laminated poster/promotional image for The New RenaisCAnce featuring eye-wear by Felicity Jury-Cramp and jewellery by Sophie Harley." **page two hundred and thirteen**

project magazine page. **title _Dead Fuel_. designers Peter Miles, Damon Murray, Stephen Sorrell. design company/stylists Fuel. client _Fuel_ magazine. year 1993. photographer Peter Anderson.** project magazine page. **title _Grey Fuel_. designers Peter Miles, Damon Murray, Stephen Sorrell. design company/stylists Fuel. client _Fuel_ magazine. year 1994. photographer Juergen Teller. comment** "Fuel created a strong corporate image for themselves by adopting the uniform of the establishment, bespoke three-piece suits. They wanted to prove they meant business. While working on _Grey_, Fuel intended to include an image of a transvestite, a grey area of sexuality. Instead they decided to lampoon themselves, and show their detractors that they do possess a sense of humour by commissioning tailored pinafore dresses reminiscent of a school-girl's uniform." **page two hundred and fifteen**

10×5

projects invitation, catalogue, exhibition. **title 10x5 fashion. designers Stephen Turner, James Hodgson, Chris Turner. design company 10x5. client 10x5 = Public. year 1995. comment** "ten images were contributed by the original five members of the group, commenting on the meaning of fashion. The shirt, made of un-tearable paper, is the invitation. The photographic images are of a swing tag found in the street and a clock salvaged from a family member's garage." **page two hundred and seventeen**

Having picked a number i tie the chrome key close to my pre-pubital body. Cold bleach,screaming voices echo through tiled filled rooms.A wet open space awaits.'Last length',they can go soon,i look through the glass, them fully clothed,me half naked,but once i've packed my sodden bag & viewed my tight pale face,i too will be able too buy treats from the vending machine. I see Dad reading a paper, i know he watches,but never when i watch him.Windows are wet, figures outside peer in whilst out walking the Sunday dog,the misty outline forms an eerie viewing presence. I clutch at my cap in fear, the orange reflection glazes my eyes, sickening smell persists as does the collage of voices which can be heard without being present. The hesitation as it burns my scalp,my eyes become taught. Now my fear is contained beneath the rubber skin. I stand closer to the edge,wet tiles with hair str-ung between each joint. Bobbing heads travel back and forth in time too retching mouths of water. Two hour session. Maureen now becomes a rippled blur beneath the surface,her disjointed voice is the only connection with reality.

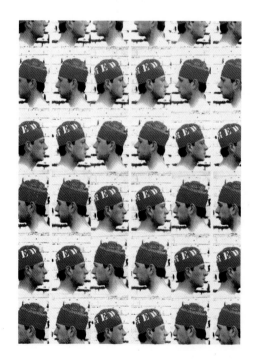

Dr Martens

projects invitation, exhibition. **title red. design
company 10x5. year 1994. text** "the exhibition was about the swimming cap as a fashion accessory. One of the designer's earliest memories
of the colour red was his red swimming cap. The caps inscribed with the story were suspended in glass tanks of water. The invitation
was a cap sealed in a foil pack." project t-shirt design. **design company 10x5. client Dr Martens. year 1995. page two hundred and nineteen**

project t-shirt designs. title genuine gear, DR brand, DR spaceman, DR vampireman,
DR sokka! design company/illustrators/typographers/stylists The Designers Republic. years 1993-1995. page two hundred and twenty one

projects t-shirt design, image from press release. **title prick t-shirt. designers AL.W, Simon B Babaloo. design company AL.W. year 1994. press release text** "an explanation. With skate gear currently being the hip street wear, there's plenty of bad signals being given off by the nouveaux millionaires running the scene. One particularly foul, bad, tasteless t-shirt comes from Sal Rocco and has a man pointing a gun at a woman's head with the word 'bitch' over the top, dodgy as fuck. Subverting the controversial 'bitch' t-shirt, Manchester-based video makers AL.W and Simon B Babaloo hit back with a 'prick' t-shirt.

'The prick is an English take on the bitch t-shirt, a sucker punch at the crappy casual sexism of the skateboard scene and the t-shirt which I thought could be misinterpreted,' claims AL.W. In the tradition of subverting big-time companies by bootlegging and subtly altering their codes, AL.W has come up with a snappy take on the t-shirt. On the top it says 'prick' and the female is pointing the gun at the man. Sal Rocco's brother Steve runs World Industries – possibly the world's largest skateboarding manufacturer. He was involved in a skate team called Girl whose members left to skate for a team elsewhere. The 'bitch' t-shirt was an attempt to hit back at them, but the wider context makes it seem like a slimy, sexist comment." **comment** "the pictogram for male and female toilets is here used to spell out the most blatant of messages about the dangers of sexism."

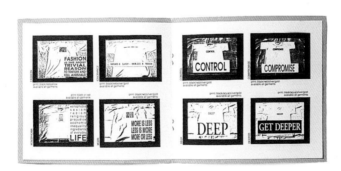

project t-shirt. title free. designer Marlo. design company Marlo 23. client retail. year 1995. project mail order catalogue. **designer Marlo. design company Marlo 23. year 1995. press release text** "what is Marlo 23? We make and sell our own naturally-based t-shirts, clothing and knitwear. We have grown, assembling an understated range of garments; simple, sound cuts supporting the adage that less really is more. We use only the eco-friendliest materials we can find; re-cycled/re-spun cotton, rayon, denim...as well as our latest shapes in hemp and various hemp/re-cycled material mixes. The textile industry is responsible for much environmental degradation, animal and human oppression and simply haphazard consumption and waste. Our garments address these situations, from the suppliers of our raw materials to our donations to environmental and compassionate organisations. We evolved whilst travelling in Australia during 1988 to 1990; moving around, selling our t-shirts with didactic messages containing our fundamental ethos. Since our return to the UK we have been based in St Ives, Cornwall, and this summer completed a commission to design and print the official Tate Gallery shirt. Media coverage has resulted in a global clientele. We have a commitment to work for change, promoting lifestyles that are free from exploitation of animals and people. We now know that we share this 'seductive ideology'." **page two hundred and twenty three**

project range of merchandise. **title American Retro. designer Mervyn Rands. design company Penrose Design Limited. client American Retro. comment** "graphic designer Mervyn Rands produced an identity for American Retro which has been applied to a range of merchandise along with the words 'Soho, London' creating an instantly recognisable product with international cachet." project window display, American Retro, London. **title road signs. year 1995. photographer Andy Hughes. page two hundred and twenty five**

t-shirts. **title road sign shirts (emotional zone, give in, think). designer David Fryer. client American Retro. year 1995.** project packaging, cufflinks. **title highway code. designer/typographer Lydia Thornley. client Simon Carter. year 1995. comment** "familiar, easy to read graphic devices are reappropriated because they have proven ability as communication devices. Traffic signs can stop you in your tracks." project hold-all. **title bomb. designer David Fryer. client American Retro. year 1995. comment** "a subversive appropriation of the classic Pan Am logo reminds us that the threat of terrorism is constant, not just while flying, but also on the streets of London." **page two hundred and twenty seven**

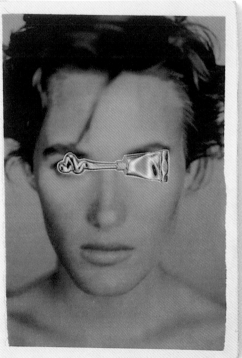

project t-shirt. **title keep the world tidy. designer**
Judy Blame. agent Gimme 5 Limited. project note books. designer/stylist Judy Blame. quote Judy Blame "I make books up all the time with
different visuals. I have hundreds of these and they are like my dictionaries. I just rip things out of magazines, jot down people's names, and
I take them to meetings and then, say, Neneh Cherry might say, 'I like that, I like that, that sounds good' and we build up a direction with it. I
work with Michael Nash, they do all my graphics if I can help it, because Stephanie knows how to read my mind and Tony knows how to put it
down technically. I can just say something…and, because I'm not classically trained in anything really – I couldn't cut a pattern or work a
computer to save my life – I'm kind of like the liaison person, putting the team together. I have a problem with a job description.
When I styled Björk for *Debut* I didn't want to disguise her I wanted to advertise
her. Music styling is about being inspired by the people. The thing about styling, and a lot of stylists working in the music business forget
this, you can't put an outfit on someone if it doesn't suit them, but when you know something will suit someone you recommend it, it's got
to look believable, you've got to think about the character of the person and what they can get away with." **page two hundred and twenty nine**

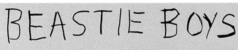

project t-shirt. **title hyperformance. designer Haze. design company Haze Productions. agent Gimme 5 Limited. year 1994.** project 12" record cover. **title** *so what 'cha want*. **designer Haze. design company Haze Productions. client The Beastie Boys. agent Gimme 5 Limited. year 1994. quote Eric Haze** "I started out as an artist in New York, it was a big art scene back in the early 1970s. I started with graffiti which was still all about the written word at that point and it stayed underground without getting any recognition until about 1980 when a group of us called the Soul Artists consciously made an effort to bring the elements together and make it more of an art movement with a purpose. By the mid-1980s, the art scene in New York had died out. I was able to make a transition into music as an arena for my art, partly because hip hop and the culture came up together, rap music eclipsed art as the medium of the moment, so when everyone wanted to be an artist and open galleries in the early 1980s, everyone wanted to be a musician and start record labels in the late 1980s and it provided an outlet for the work, and a learning curve. The beauty of it, and the reason I became a graphic designer rather than an artist, is that record covers provided a more populist outlet for the work. I subscribe to the notion of low art rather than high art and, like with the trains, you can do one piece and it travels the city to ten million people, there is a parallel populist notion with album covers. Instead of one person owning your painting for $100,000, 100,000 people can own your work for $1, and philosophically and politically, that's the natural progression to clothing, being a direct outlet as a pop medium with mass production, not placing the emphasis on the individual piece but having mass appeal, that's not a dirty word." project logo sketches. **designer Haze. year early 1980s. quote Eric Haze** "the essense of a great logo is that it looks like you've seen it for years but you've never seen it before. If you can get that timeless quality, whether you're ripping off something and making it new or grabbing the essence of various things that you can't necessarily put your finger on, it's retro and futuristic at the same time. If you can get that tension going then it's not going to look dated in a year."

title Björk t-shirts, violently happy, venus as a boy. design company Me Company. client Winterland. year 1994. quote Paul White, Me Company "one of the original ideas was that we'd have at least two t-shirts released a month, that would be hybrids of the logo, short runs, 500 each, out to the shops, sold, gone, more more. People buying them begin to see them as limited-editions that won't come round again. I like the fact that that makes people want them, it makes it worth going into a shop to look because there is going to be something different there. Out on tour, on a couple of specific dates, they sold about 2,000 over three gigs, there have been large quanitites of this stuff sold. But I think these things should be small, they're just small pockets of ideas you shove out, they ripple out and are gone, and you just keep doing this, you keep pulsing these ideas out." project Björk feature.

title army of her *The Face* **June 1995. art director Lee Swillingham. designers/typographers Lee Swillingham, Stuart Spalding. photographer Andrea Giacobbe. stylist Joanna Thaw. hair Gari Gianasi. make-up Cathy Lomax. quote Judy Blame** "I just happened to introduce Hussein Chalayan to Björk and she wears his clothes twenty-four hours a day, she's become his biggest client." **page two hundred and thirty one**

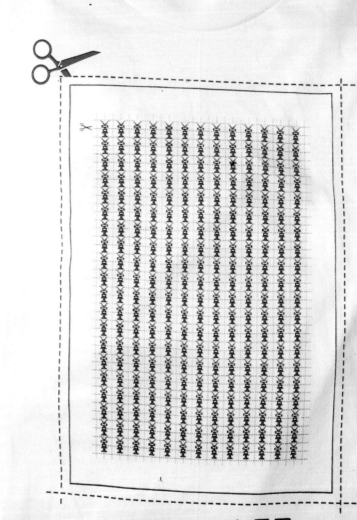

project t-shirt. title abducted. designer Gabriel Hunter. client Liquid Sky D-sign. year 1994. project mail order catalogue. designer Heather "Aquasonic" S. client Liquid Sky D-sign. year 1994. catalogue text "Liquid Sky D-Sign is a small company based in New York City Babylon. We are a team of DJs, musicians, fashion designers, writers, poets, multi-media artists. We believe in friends, music, lovers, and the positive vibration of this universe. We are dreamers of this collective dream – reality! Promote peace and love thru underground parties! One love saves the day." project club flyer. title jungle sky. client Carlos Soul Slinger. year 1994. project t-shirt. title LSD sign. designer C-Rey. client Liquid Sky D-sign. year 1994. projects logo, promotional posters, sticker, snowboards, t-shirts. title XXX. designer/typographer Carlos Segura. design company Segura Inc. client XXX Snowboards. year 1995. photographer Jeff Sciortino. page two hundred and thirty three

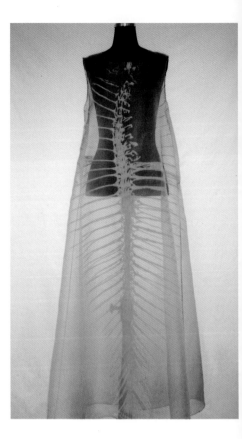

to eat + to cloth

Das ist eine Einladung
zu einem visuell
kulinarischem
Schauessen am
Samstag,
den 17. September
ab 14.00 Uhr
im Garten von
Patricia und
Renée Hepp.

Gotthelfstraße 53
81677 München
Telefon 089 915589

Wir freuen uns
auf Eure Gesellschaft.

nicht nur Sack und Mampf

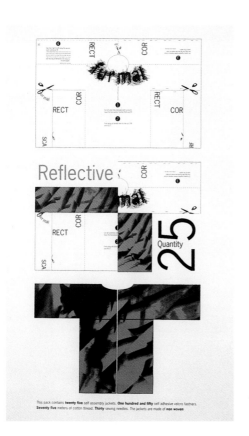

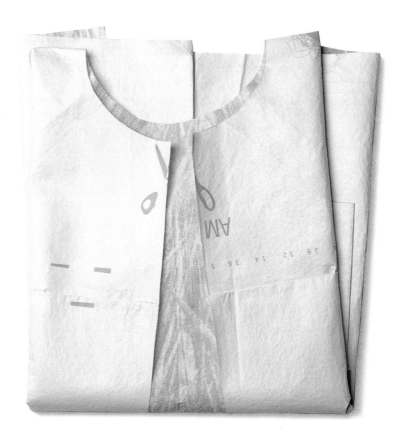

projects invitation, event, documentation. **title to eat + to clothe. concept/designer/maker of clothes Patricia Hepp. photographer Shoheia Staffler. hair/make-up Beate Niebler. choreographer Antonia Arboleda. text** "in this project I connected food and clothes together with an event. It took place in Munich in a green-house at a market garden on 17 September 1994. There was a dinner for about twenty guests. With every new course that was served, a new guest arrived, wearing an appropriate dress. This necessitated that the senses of seeing and tasting were involved at the same time. Parallel delights." project informative clothing. **title the furmal jacket. designers/photographers/typographers George Lewis, David Revell. design company LewisRevell. year 1994. comment** "instructions for how to make the jacket are printed onto the actual paper/fabic garment." **page two hundred and thirty five**

project machine-knitted jersey jacket.
title nosy sony. designer Charlene Mullen. design company Fecit Design. year 1991. photographer Charlene Mullen. project range of belts.
title cubist hamburger. designer Stevie King. design company S-Tek. year 1989. quote Stevie King "the whole issue of environmentalism and ecology is to do with more is less. You can produce 25 cheap belts and they last six months and fall to pieces or else they're fashion belts and out of fashion, but I'm saying, 'no, you only need one belt, and it gets better as it gets older, therefore you don't have to kill as many cows, you don't have to melt as much metal, you don't have to use so much energy and the ultimate dream was that everybody would have one and then I'd go out of business. I really like the idea that Galileo was put in prison for saying the world was round and I always thought that was quite an amazing thing that at a particular point in history we said the world was flat and now it's round. I did the moons and stars and suns and the alchemy belts and that whole thing was preparation for the situation I'm in now, in that I am understanding change, because I knew that's the way of the future and you have to be able to change yourself in order to learn to cope with the fact that the whole system is breaking down. The belts don't actually symbolise change. I was reading about change at the time and these things came out of it, these symbols of the trident for quick lime or cement for the money hunters stabbing money, the urban spiral, the cubist hamburger.
It's to do with searching for new values
as well as change, and it's saying that the value system that we've got is shit, it doesn't work and I don't believe in it because there are a disproportionate number of people who are unhappy to those that are happy. Has it ever been different at any other time in history? Well, yes it has actually and what if...? The cubist hamburger, that's the bun at the bottom and at the top and the hole is the nutritional food value that is missing after McDonald's have cut down all the trees, got the meat off the bones with air hoses and sludged it into cubes. That is all about the value that is removed by the heavy processing of our society, and that symbol's out of my head, it's a combination, a fusion, it's about what's missing and that's what we're all looking for and it's about square pegs in round holes." **page two hundred and thirty seven**

BRICK: FIRST FLOOR 2B AGAR GROVE CAMDEN TOWN LONDON NW1 9TD 0171 267 2196
T-SHIRT '31.JUN.1995' 50 LIMITED EDITION £19 PER ITEM CHEQUES PAYABLE TO M.GOLDIE

THE ULTIMATE GROOVING MACHINE.

project t-shirt. **title meat is shit. designers Tim Goldie, Malcolm Goldie. design company Ceramic Rabbit. typographer Malcolm Goldie. year 1993. text on swing tag** "deconstructosystemmns high tension t-shirt concrete. this garment-nutrient will burst into flames 18 days 42 minutes after purchase. 84% chance that tag contains hidden microscopic molten information & hydraulicaustic vibro diagrams (within second & third or eighth layer). send a stamp for full catalogue, stickers, powder and other drooling fragments." project print ad. **title Brick '31 June 1995'** *i-D* July 1995. **designers Malcolm Goldie, Paul Blackburn. design company Brick. year 1995.** project t-shirts. **title prostitutes' phone box cards. designers A Holland, D Holliday. design company Trouble. year 1994.** project t-shirt. **title touch. design company Nice. client Esprit. year 1993.** project t-shirt. **title BMW groove machine, menswear mainline collection. designer Toby Benjamin. design company 303 Culture Limited. year 1995. comment** "the A303 is the route taken by travellers going to Stonehenge, Glastonbury and the west country." **page two hundred and thirty nine**

BRIAN BADERMAN "I STARTED TO WRITE LOTS OF LITTLE STORIES FOR THE CATALOGUE
TO COVER. SO IT GETS TO BE REALLY DENSE, BUT THAT'S KIND OF ME REALLY, LIKE SO
KIND OF PICK UP A SENSE OF CONCERN WHEN GRAPHIC DESIGNERS TALK ABOUT
CATALOGUE, MAKES PEOPLE LAUGH. BUT WHY MAKE PEOPLE LAUGH? BECAUSE FAS
SCHIZOPHRENIC HUMOUR. THEN I'M HAPPY." STEPHANIE NASH, MICHAEL NASH "AN AF
AND WHAT WOMEN BUY, WHICH I DON'T KNOW. IT'S A WHOLE DIFFERENT EXPERT
COMMERCIAL PIECE FROM THE COLLECTION, BECAUSE IT MAKES A REALLY GOOD SHAF
SURE THEY'RE SHOT." TERRY JONES, INSTANT DESIGN "I THINK THERE ARE LOADS OF
FAIR. WE HAD A TRUCK-LOAD OF CLOTHES AND PEOPLE COULD CHOOSE WHETHER T
1960S AND 1970S. IT'S DIFFICULT TO KNOW WHICH COMES FIRST. I THINK A LOT OF T
INVOLVED IN FASHION, CREATING THE IMAGES PART OF THE PROCESS, YOUR ROLE IS
THAT FASHION WAS BEING PRESENTED I FELT WASN'T RELEVANT BECAUSE I THOUGH
WOULD TRY TO GET PHOTOGRAPHERS WHO TREATED THE MODELS AS HUMAN BEING
ABOUD SODANO "I RUN EVERY PIECE OF GRAPHIC OUTPUT WORLD-WIDE. WHATEVER W
ARE PRIMARILY FOR THE JAPANESE MARKET AND TAILORED TO THEIR REQUIREMENTS
CATALOGUES, 15,000 FOR THE JAPANESE MARKET. WE ALSO OFFER THE GRAPHICS S
OUT ALL THE MATERIAL FROM HERE." JUDY BLAME "WHAT HAPPENED IN LONDON, WH
AND GOING 'I'VE GOT A WICKED STORY'...PEOPLE LIKE RAY PETRI, AMANDA GRIEVE, D
WORKED FOR A MAGAZINE YOU HAD NOWHERE. IT WAS ALL ABOUT IDEAS AND CREATI
FIRST YOHJI YAMAMOTO CATALOGUE IN 1986 MARC ASCOLI SAID TO ME 'WHY DON'T Y
'LET'S DO SOMETHING CORRESPONDING TO THE WAY NICK KNIGHT SHOOTS IT, AN
LAYOUT. IMAGINE A PARTY IN A WHITE ROOM AND YOU'RE PANNING A CAMERA ARO
DESIGNER CLOTHING FOR MEN IN MARCH 1991 WAS THAT IT HAD ALL BECOME A W
PLATEAU THAT SOMEHOW HAD TO KEEP PUMPING UP. I THOUGHT THAT IF I COULD GET
MIGHT SAY, 'WELL AT LEAST YOHJI STILL HAS HIS FINGER ON THE PULSE'." ROBIN DEF
PHOTOGRAPHERS WHO WORK FOR ALL THE BEST MAGAZINES WORLD-WIDE. I HAVE TO
TELL THE WORLD, THAT BIBA SYMBOL, I STILL OWN THAT, AND I'VE NOTICED THEY'RE I
ANYTHING TO DO WITH FASHION. 'THIS IS WONDERFUL'...I DON'T UNDERSTAND HOW A
WORDS ALLOW THAT TO HAPPEN." HUSSEIN CHALAYAN "I SEE CLOTHES AS GRAPHIC
FORMS, AND THE FACT THAT THEY CAN BE PHOTOGRAPHED AS A THING ON A WALL
LONDON AND IF I HAD A CAMERA I'M SURE I COULD TAKE 30 STRAIGHT-UPS, NO PROE
BE THE SAME. IT'S OUR KIND OF STYLE TO BE UP-FRONT AND ON THE STREET ABOUT
THE MOST COMPELLING, BEAUTIFUL WOVEN LABEL HAS TO BE MARGIELA'S WHITE ON
ON THE NATURE OF FASHION." BRIAN BADERMAN "THE LAYOUT FOR THE DIESEL CA
DISTRIBUTED FROM THERE, THE PRINT RUN IS 500,000, IN ONE LANGUAGE. CAN
LANGUAGE. I'M NOT VERY INTERESTED IN GRAPHICS. A LOT OF GRAPHICS ARE OVER-D
THEN YOU LOOK AT IT A YEAR OR TWO LATER AND IT SEEMS A STYLE AND NOT A LOT M
WANT TO PUT THEIR CREATIVE FINGER IN. CONTROLLING THAT CREATIVITY IS THE H
"BJÖRK HAS A HOME PAGE ON THE WEB WHICH WE WERE INVOLVED IN SETTING UP FO
CYBER GIRL SHIRT, WITH THE WORLD WIDE WEB ADDRESS ON THE BACK. IT'S AVAILAB
IT IS CURRENTLY THROUGH SNAIL MAIL, BUT IT'S PRETTY MUCH AVAILABLE WORLD-WI
NOT WITH A PR AGENCY, AND WITH YVONNE SPORRE AS ART DIRECTOR. SHE'S VERY
DIRECTIONS. SHE HAS AN IDEA AND WE REALISE IT, WE DISCUSS IDEAS TOGETHE